# Way Down Deep
## in the Belly
## of the Beast

*Travels by Night: A Memoir of the Sixties*
*The File on Arthur Moss*
*Selected Poems*
*The Dreams of Ancient Peoples*
*Variorum: New Poems and Old 1965–1985*
*Moving towards the Vertical Horizon*
*Rites of Alienation*
*Chinese Anthology*
*The Blue Notebook: Reports on Canadian Culture*
*Notes from a Journal*
*The Five Lives of Ben Hecht*
*The Crowded Darkness*
*Some Day Soon: Essays on Canadian Songwriters*
*Year of the Horse: A Journey through Russia and China*
*Gold Diggers of 1929*
*The Gold Crusades: A Social History of Gold Rushes*
    *1849–1929*
*The Rise of the Canadian Newspaper*
*A Little Bit of Thunder*
*The Other China*
*Documents in Canadian Art* (editor)

# Way Down Deep in the Belly of the Beast

## Douglas Fetherling

A Memoir

of the

Seventies

McArthur & Company

Toronto

This paperback edition published in 2001
by McArthur & Company
322 King Street West, Suite 402
Toronto, ON M5V 1J2

First published by Lester Publishing, 1996

**National Library of Canada Cataloguing in Publication Data**

Fetherling, George, 1949—
  Way down deep in the belly of the beast: a memoir of the seventies

ISBN 1-55278-195-X

1. Fetherling, George, 1949—    . 2. London (England) — Intellectual life –
20th century. 3. Toronto (Ont.) — Intellectual life — 20th century. 4. Authors,
Canadian (English) — 20th century — Bibliography.* I. Title.

PS8561.E834Z54 2001          C811'.54          C2001-930159-6
PR9199.3.F475Z478 2001

Text design: Gordon Robertson

Printed and bound in Canada by Transcontinental

The publisher would like to acknowledge the financial support
of the Government of Canada through the Book Publishing
Industry Development Program (BPIDP) for our publishing
activities. The publisher further wishes to acknowledge the
financial support of the Ontario Arts Council for our
publishing program.

10 9 8 7 6 5 4 3 2 1

# Contents

# London
## by Twilight

SOMETIMES when it rains I get nostalgia in my joints. The rain had been coming down hard through the night of November 17, 1989, when the last newspapers to be printed in Fleet Street came off the monstrous Goss presses at the *Daily Express* building, the so-called Black Lubyanka at No. 121, where Lord Beaverbrook once disported himself so merrily, drunk with intrigue and conspiracy. The last newspaper staff with offices in the Street, that of the *Daily Mail*, had decamped several months earlier. November 17, however, would mark the absolute and final end of the tradition, one both noble and ignoble, that started in 1702 when the *Daily Courant* began printing in what its last two generations of inhabitants were amused to call the Street of Shame. I was on my annual visit back to London at the time, and so the following morning I took a stroll there with my friend Daniel Williman, who had come down from Oxford for this purpose. Dan is another sucker for ceremony.

The itinerary was as familiar as it was simple, for this was part of my past from the twilight of Swinging London. The route was for years my favourite walk, one I had taken in all weathers. I may very well continue to enjoy it, for though it always leaves me bewildered and with a sense of what's been lost, it also gives me little glimpses of the future, showing London not as a museum but as an organism, alive with its own continuity.

Dan and I began in Trafalgar Square, where there is usually a protest demonstration under way. That morning's involved ambulance drivers who were on strike. Pigeons protested against the protesters. To the left, in Cockspur Street, where all the steamship companies used to reside, Canada House stood a little decrepitly, cross-hatched with scaffolding; to the right was South Africa House, with the customary pickets out front, denouncing apartheid (which would soon come to an end—who would have thought that life would so improve in South Africa while getting worse in Canada?). The bells of St-Martin's-in-the-Fields rang out above the traffic. I told Dan it was good to hear that they still peal. In Thatcherite Britain, London's Georgian churches found themselves devoting more and more of their meagre energies to taking up the slack in social and cultural services, making do as shelters, theatres, drop-in centres, crisis centres, job markets, food banks, data banks, hotlines and lifelines. St Martin's, however, had gone an equal distance in the other direction. The crypt by this time had become a pricey café, where people scuffed their shoes on the eighteenth-century gravestones laid side by side to make trendy flooring.

Even more so than a year or two previously, London, on what was probably, for me, my last meaningful visit there, the last one in which I had a personal stake based on memory, seemed defined by the tension between gentrification and its opposite. We set off up St Martin's Lane (intending to pause at a rather good restaurant called the Pelican, much patronized by writers and actors—a thing unknown in my day) and poked about a bit in Covent Garden. There was now a whole generation, complete in every particular, that didn't remember when the name was synonymous with the produce market, just as their offspring probably won't associate Fleet Street with journalism. I tried to describe to Dan the smashed vegetable crates and the loose leaves of lettuce that used to litter the pavement, how the chefs from the big hotels would find their way there at dawn to do their buying for the day, and how that one pub had special dispensation to keep ungodly hours so that the hawkers and the people behind the big iron-wheeled barrows could get a drink at 9:00 a.m.

"There used to be a little block of flats, a very plain façade, perhaps about twelve feet wide," I said. Maybe it's still there but tarted up to match all the boutiques. A friend of a friend from Vancouver lived there in a place he sublet from a famous actress who was away on an extended tour. "The owner's bed," I recalled, "was on a sort of throne, which one approached via a short flight of stairs on three sides." Dan, who is a medievalist, cited a number of precedents for this sort of interior design. We circled back and entered Charing Cross Road, passing all the bookshops along the east side of the street (the west side having been razed sometime in the 1970s and replaced with a great long unintentional example of Toronto-style architecture—Torontoesque grotesque). Dan was polite but incredulous, the way people must be listening to armchair fly-fishermen, when I told him my story of finding a proof copy of *Under Milk Wood* some twenty years ago for ten bob, the only large-scale sleeper I've ever found in Charing X or indeed anywhere in the whole country.

At Cambridge Circus, where a permanent electronic sign for *Cats* or something had replaced the one I remembered for Danny LaRue, the female-impersonator extraordinaire, we bore right, into Shaftesbury Avenue. It at least remained reassuringly theatrical, with costumers' shops and agents' offices. And so into Theobalds Road, which I'm certain must once have been pronounced Thibbalds, since Alexander Pope uses the name somewhere to rhyme with *ribald*.

After Gray's Inn Road, where the first Lord Thomson moved the *Sunday Times* (two moves ago now), we came to Clerkenwell Road, and I was in my old stomping ground, EC1. Every old building in London that wasn't at that exact moment being replaced was either collapsing or being beautifully restored. Such was certainly the case here along this stretch, where enormous commercial structures from the last part of the previous century, imposing in their sheer greyness, were either boarded up and full of rubbish or else buzzing with workers who kept bumping into the draped tarpaulins like incompetent actors who can't find the opening in the curtain.

Farther along, the street becomes more residential, with Victorian mansion flats with uncountable chimney-pots. There are also rows of little shops, every conceivable kind, which make you think at once that Napoleon (quoting Adam Smith) was correct, a nation of shopkeepers indeed. Within the grasp of my doddering memory this was a white working-class neighbourhood where you could buy Woodbines in packets of three from Tom Cornish Tobacconist (by the 1980s a chain store, with only a faded rectangle where old Tom's portrait used to hang). Now the area had changed in two ways. It had become home to many people of East Indian and Caribbean origin, and it also had gone somewhat upscale.

My old slum with the shilling meter looked to have become a condo. No doubt at all about the corner launderette, where kindly neighbourhood women right out of the cast of *EastEnders* had taught me what combinations of colours could safely be washed together in Daz detergent. It was now the inevitable bistro (most definitely not an old-fashioned kaff), serving nouvelle cuisine to adults who cultivate the anorexic look.

Just beyond lay Farringdon Road, where so many were killed in the Blitz. The top part of it was also an area in transition by this time, a sort of artisans' quarter in the making, full of small publishers' and ad agencies' offices hacked out of what were once warehouses or light industrial plants. Clerkenwell Close was where a shortlived newspaper, the *Sunday Correspondent*, had chosen to locate. We cut down towards Fleet Street in search of that other area and another era.

There was no market in Leather Lane that day, and the absence of a crowd only emphasized the changes, the buildings taken down for car parks or for other, worse buildings. Across Holborn and into Fetter Lane, which keeps turning up in the *Newgate Calendar* and eighteenth-century broadsides as the scene of unspeakable crimes. Fetter Lane at least still bore a few signs of being devoted to a profession that has been reinvigorated but, as a result, had moved away. The Printer's Devil pub, I thought out loud, will soon be a name without context. And then, ta-da, we entered Fleet Street, wishing for all the world that we were seeing it as, say, Sir Philip Gibbs encountered it originally, with people stepping carelessly into the flow of omnibuses and horse-drawn paper wagons.

The clock on the *Daily Telegraph* building was stuck at twelve o'clock and no doubt had been since Conrad Black moved the paper to the Isle of Dogs. In contrast, the other proprietors seemed to have taken even their signage with them. I thought I knew what was what from the time when I was the world's most unsuccessful freelance writer. (*Plus ça change*, I could hear Dan saying to himself.) But for the life of me it was confusing now, as though I were the Germans and the Home Guard had taken down all the road signs to confound me. Wasn't the *Liverpool Echo* building the black grimy one over there? I was no longer sure.

I was somewhat heartened to see that St-Dunstan'sin-the-West, whose pastoral mission centred on the generally unsalvageable souls of journalists and printers, had not been made into a nightclub (it looked too forlorn ever to be a nightclub) and that down towards Ludgate Hill the famous bookshop to which all the world's review copies once gravitated was still there, though trade seemed to go forward at the pace of rapidly cooling lava. But the kaff called Mick's (or The Mick's, as I'd heard it called by bigots, for the foul-tempered proprietor was an Irishman) was shuttered for good. I imagine it was not, as Mick might have feared, a victim of the practice of extending credit to newspeople but rather of the removal of the opportunity to continue doing so.

The dome of St Paul's sat in the distance like an enormous melon, and we were drawn there, Dan and I, by the eighteenth-century graffiti carved into the columns outside and by the tombs of Wellington and Chinese Gordon within and by Holman Hunt's painting *The Light of the World*, a copy he made of the one in Keble College Chapel, Oxford. Personally, I find it impossible to look up at those galleries or down along the great expanse of floor to the altar and not be moved—despite myself when I was young, reassuringly so now that I'm not.

At my urging, Dan, whose own sympathies are with Rome and who is an authority on church architecture and numerous other topics, discoursed on the many specifically Catholic features that survived Henry VIII and his influence.

"This is one," he said, looking around a last time, "that I insist still belongs to us."

And so, as Pepys might have said, we betook ourselves to lunch.

———

Twenty years earlier, when the Swinging London of
contemporary legend was still in session, there was no
better metropolis in which to waste one's youth.
Amsterdam may have offered more licence, but no
other place matched London's combination of
licence, social mobility and civility, or so it seemed for
a while. The cream of the world's young people
appeared to have come together there. Or if not the
cream, then the most colourful and representative
sampling. The capital had been taken over by a tribe
(an overworked word of the time) dressed in strange
and outrageous native attire, much of it donned in
affectionate ridicule of the recent past.

I knew from what I had read and felt that the
1950s had got under way in some official sense with
the Festival of Britain in 1951, an exposition whose
forced tone of optimism no one really believed—and
rightly so, for in the fifties the privations of war
remained so close in time that rationing, for instance,
was still a fact of life. According to the cultural calendar, the 1960s probably began with the Profumo
Scandal of 1963, not because it brought down the
Macmillan Conservatives, but because it was, after
all, a *sex* scandal, seasoned with hints of drugs and
espionage: its very nature seemed to proclaim the
old decade's death. So the London of the later
1960s and early 1970s was a rebirth and a funeral

rolled into one—a wake of sorts, and the wildest of its kind.

London had survived the terror of the Second World War but continued to bear some of the scars. Within actual sight of Piccadilly Circus, at the spot in Shaftesbury Avenue where I used to queue for a late-night bus, hoardings still hid rubble left by the German bombing. Yet though London had come out of the doldrums (with a vengeance), it had yet to be ruined by the excessive money-grubbing of later times. The still-new Post Office Tower, as it was then called, was the only hideously ugly structure defacing the skyline, if such a term as *skyline* could be applied to what remained physically, in its commercial as well as its domestic architecture, an almost wholly Victorian city—that is, when it was not actually Georgian.

Sir Peter Ustinov once told me a story about his late friend Charles Laughton who, when preparing to depart for Hollywood to play Captain Bligh in *Mutiny on the Bounty*, had paused at Gieves, the naval tailors in Old Bond Street, to have his uniforms made. The tailor dumbfounded him by disappearing into the cellar and returning with the mannequin of the real William Bligh (died 1817), a slender, rather un-Laughton-like man, apparently, whose measurements were kept to hand in case he should ever reorder. The London I found on fleeing Toronto was full of such eccentricities. You could still stand at Bank tube station and see the double lines of identical men in bowlers carrying rolled brollies descending the stairs on their way to jobs in the City, just as Eliot had described them in "The Waste Land." Yet freaks and heads also wore old bowlers, to say nothing of discarded band uniforms, regimental sashes and bits of military tack, even boas. London was the perfect venue for a costume party, a perpetual masquerade convened to celebrate individual freedom.

Everybody came, some in such devil-may-care second-hand clothes from the cheapest market stalls, but others done up in the more calculated retro-style from Biba's in Kensington High Street. Some people affected Moroccan caftans and jhelabas (they were the aesthetes), while others (the tourists) made do with mass-produced mod gear from shops like the one called I Was Lord Kitchener's Valet or (heaven forbid) Carnaby Street. Personally, my own centre of fashion gravity was the period immediately before the outbreak of the Great War. I found this fertile ground for inexpensive ostentation. I blush to say that I owned not one but two cloaks. The first was an old bobby's cape with lion's-head closures at the throat, purchased at the lower (cheaper) end of Portobello Road and guaranteed to elicit stern looks from real bobbies on the beat. The second, also blue, was longer, fuller, infinitely brighter, lined in some satin-like material that suggested the inside of a burial-society coffin.

But London was not only a carnival for lithe young bodies, it was a feast for famished minds like mine. In a way that I think of as typical of that time and generation, I petered away a great deal of energy in the almost always unsuccessful attempt to make myself appealing to young women named Fiona who shared flats in Chelsea with other young women named Penelope. If one were genuinely hot (I never was, of course), one might meet someone who was hyphen-ated, someone known by some such appellation as Felicity Salmon-Trout. If one were impossibly lucky, one might actually make the acquaintance of a hyphenated person whose parents lived in a house with a hyphenated name in a hyphenated village: Felicity Salmon-Trout, Bull-in-Chinashop, Hye-upon-Drugs, Hertfordshire. In retrospect, my behaviour seems a childish acquiescence to loneliness if also, looking back, typical of that important but all-too-narrow window between the marketing of the birth-control pill and the start of the AIDS epidemic: fifteen years of liberty and experiment, more or less. (A stray fact I've just remembered: condoms were customarily purchased only at men's hairdressers. Why do I recall this, given that nobody I knew used condoms and that, in any event, I cut my own hair?)

Readers younger than myself may have difficulty appreciating the great blast of energy sent shooting through society by the start of the contemporary women's movement, surely the most fundamentally important socio-political event of our time and one especially interesting to observe at that early point, when the U.S. approach to women's issues had not yet obscured the British and European and when there was as yet no significant element of gender separatism. Certainly the whole society was sexist to a degree that would seem unfathomable even six or seven years later. But in the pop culture, one could find flashes of a new fashion for female independence (and in a media society, such a vogue is the first prerequisite for real change). "When she's gone, she's gone," sang Paul

Simon proudly. "When she stays, she stays here." Or Mick Jagger: "She would never say where she came from . . . / While the sun is bright / or in the darkest night / no one knows: / She comes and goes."

Such images were immensely compelling, bound up, as they were, with a desire to reduce class and race barriers as well. Jagger may have sneered when he sang of a woman down on her luck, "Now she gets her kicks in Stepney, not in Knightsbridge like before." But the social traffic moved in both directions. London (of all places! how amazing!) was suddenly prehensile. It was also the laboratory of ideas, as California was merely a factory for notions. Not only the women's movement, but also the incipient gay rights movement, the environmental movement, the revival of philosophical anarchism—these were among the currents of debate. The irresistible cacophony of thinking and writing was piled atop the accumulated thought of the ages. Out for my daily stroll to the twenty-four-hour post office in Trafalgar Square, for instance, I would go along Holborn from the City and into Bloomsbury, and come to the world headquarters of the Sweden-borg Society, where they still revered the eighteenth-century divine who envisioned a complicated hierarchy in Heaven not unlike the British class system. A little farther still, in Red Lion Square, fiery Welsh nationalists existed side by side with the Diggers, who redistributed used clothing (and used food) to the thick clusters of hippies from Rotterdam or San Francisco who lolled on the steps of public buildings while, on another plane, art and money provoked each other to extremes of being.

Perfervid entrepreneurs raced up Greek, Dean, Frith and Wardour streets in Soho towards suddenly mandatory little restaurants, making film, book and record deals take form, like magicians using flash-paper to create fire with a snap of the fingers. All this was far more sophisticated than anything I'd seen in New York or Toronto. There was a sense of community (another worn-out word of the time but still evocative if used strictly). At the all-night Boots Chemists in Piccadilly Circus the most fascinating drug addicts from all strata of society would come to get their government-sanctioned maintenance doses of whatever they were hooked on—skag usually, sometimes cut with rhetoric. I knew a busker who claimed to have sold his head to the University of Wales at Aberystwyth (payment in advance, of course), as the perfect specimen of the Welsh skull. I knew someone who stole for a living, going from one market barrow to another, as well as a number of casino lizards.

Parties during this period often featured a somewhat less than effulgent member of the still extant, still decadent aristocracy. He was called Binky (no, seriously), and he was, as he would always explain, soft in the head from falling off his polo pony. Eventually, during one of Binky's stays in hospital, a U.S. adventuress—an Americaness, as Bernard Shaw used to say—married him and thus married into the family estate as well.

"Can't recall a damn thing of the wedding," Binky would report good-naturedly. "I was concussed at the time actually."

At one point, my best friends outside Grub Street

were a group (bevy? coven?) of sophisticated Knights-bridge prostitutes who lived (and sometimes worked) communally, in a lovely flat in Basil Street, practically in the shadow of Harrods. There were five of them, but at any given time a couple would be out of the country escorting some gent, pol or celebrity to Hongkong or Buenos Aires. This was several years before the first great international energy crisis created by the OPEC cartel, but Arab money was already becoming prominent in London. Men in burnouses patronized the tony shops, and a new mosque had gone up near Park Lane. So my friends had had their place professionally decorated in mock Middle Eastern style, complete with a fresco of minarets painted across the largest wall of the main room. They were telling me their life stories, which I was trying to work up as a play. Writer-in-residence at a knocking-shop! I was proud of the trust shown me, which made me feel like Emile Zola. I still have the notes somewhere, or somewhere in my head I believe I do.

If I regret my spendthrift use of time searching for romance, I don't for a moment pine over how much I frittered away in my attempt (only slightly more successful) to fill gaps in my education and eke out a subsistence with my pen, though a cultural archaeologist would be needed to unearth the faint traces of my short career in the British writing world. I sent poems to the important little mags of the day, such as *Ambit* and *Stand*. I petitioned for small acts of patronage from the rather awful poet George MacBeth, a slender and intense fellow who controlled the purchase of literary work for BBC Radio; Canadians were said to be especially welcome at his office at Broadcasting House in Portland Place ever since he had been charmed off his Scots feet by Susan Musgrave, who was widely published in England at the time and had a British reputation quite separate from her growing renown at home. I also scoured the sordid edges of Fleet Street for whatever scraps of reviewing, or any other writing work, that might be available, even from trade magazines. The London word-market was the world's most competitive of course and I was almost totally ill-equipped to do battle in it, even though I was bilingual and could write in English as easily as in North American, as circumstances might require. I managed to keep going, with the occasional tiny windfall from scouting in the antiquarian-book world, where my magpie memory for inconsequential data served me well.

The fact that I once came down with scurvy reflects not my lack of money so much as my lack of common sense. I kept nocturnal writing hours and was thus often reduced to eating in Wimpy bars. The doctor at St Elizabeth's, where I sought treatment for my bleeding gums, called to the young medical students to gather round the examining table.

"I shouldn't think you'll be seeing this too very often," he told them.

As always, I wrote more than I was able to get published, no doubt more than was good for me. I turned out a bad novella about a young person murdered by rednecks while hitching across Canada, as well as a screenplay whose subject, I suppose, was energy—another term of the time that is difficult to translate today. But it is impossible to miss even now in the films of that period from people as different as Richard Lester and Lindsay Anderson and Michelangelo Antonioni—directors whose work we saw at the National Film Theatre, tucked neatly under Waterloo Bridge— one of the first signs, in that age before the Barbican Centre, that official culture was moving to the South Bank. Indeed, you could see all the masters of the past and present, from Eisenstein onwards, and study their grammar virtually frame by frame. This fostered the illusion in many of us that we could write for the screen.

But mainly what I wrote was diaristic poetry arising from my new existence. Publishing such poems was nearly impossible, but there was always an audience somewhere that would listen to them being read. Weekly or *ad hoc* poetry events filled a considerable amount of space in the what's-on listings of *Oz* and *IT*, the alternative newspapers. One could see and meet everyone, spanning the years from Stephen Spender (though at the time I was more interested in the work of his late father, Edward) down to Adrian Henri, the bear-like poet (and, later, painter as well). Henri had a special aura about him, being born and reared in Liverpool, a place that Allen Ginsberg, in the 1960s, had called "the center of consciousness of the universe." More precisely, Henri was a Liverpudlian of Lennon and McCartney's generation, and one of the ringleaders of the attempted multidisciplinary cultural revival in his native city. Along with Roger McGough, Brian Patten and a number of lesser figures, he had come to represent not only the spillover of the Beatles' adrenalin, but also promised the return of urban regionalism to English culture. All that was aeons ago now, but Henri has managed to grow as a writer without ever abandoning the old optimism and playfulness that were so evident when he came to London and read his postdated verse autobiographies in cellars and other tiny stages.

Personally, I liked hearing all the poets. These included Edwin Brock, not yet made known beyond Britain by his books with New Directions, who wrote ironic poems about his manacled life in advertising, and Philip Oakes, who combined being a poet with being one of the film critics of *The Sunday Times* (the sort of anomaly that appealed to me instinctively).

Sooner or later, one met all the poets simply by browsing in Bernard Stone's Turret Book Shop, then located in Kensington High Street (later in Lambs Conduit Street, WC1, where the foreigners' police station was). Other poetry venues included a room up top of the King of Bohemia, a pub in Hampstead High Street, where you could hear the precursor of what later came to be called dub, and the beloved Lamb and Flag (which had been named the Bucket of Blood when Dryden and his circle drank there). At the other extreme was the Roundhouse in Camden Town, known primarily for rock concerts.

The Roundhouse was an important institution of the period whose owner, a film producer and entrepreneur, was busily engaged attempting to put together a big international feature film of Peggy Atwood's novel *The Edible Woman*, a project that never came to fruition. Alas, I never met the indefatigable poetry editor and private press stalwart Roger

Burford Mason when I was in Britain. We became friends only after he immigrated to Canada in the late 1980s, when some chance name would drop from his tongue and suddenly bring back to me this whole milieu.

One night the National Book League (now the Book Trust) held a miniature Commonwealth poetry festival that turned out somewhat disastrously, because all the participants, as Ill luck would have it, seemed only to confirm the host nation's stereotypes of them. The principal Australian poet, for example, arrived falling-down drunk, while two African poets proved to have strong tribal hatreds that precluded their sharing the stage. There were many expat Canadians in London in those days. They ranged from Chuck Carlson of Prince George and later Vancouver, the author of *strange movies (i've seen)*, to Tom Marshall of Kingston, who had come to oversee the sale of *The Psychic Mariner*, his now seldom-cited study of D.H. Lawrence's poetry. Tom, who I'm sure will be considered one of the foremost Canadian poets of the gay sensibility, was not yet out of the closet at this time and often used Gwen MacEwen, also then in London, as his armpiece, to use the term of the homosexual underground. Atwood was in London, too, and so, more briefly, was Dennis Lee. The list makes no pretension to being comprehensive and does not include any of what seemed the permanent Canadian expats, such as Douglas Day, the all-round man-of-letters, whom I unfortunately never met. Nor George Hulme, the playwright and art collector, who hailed from Hamilton, Ontario, and whose plays were constantly being produced and published in Britain and Europe but not in Canada, where he wasn't known. George wrote the comedy *The Lionel Touch*, which lured Rex Harrison out of retirement and back to the West End; more seriously, he also wrote the controversial *Life and Death of Adolf Hitler*, which in its playing time and cast size outdid O'Neill. George lived near the south side of Sloane Square, in a flat with felted walls and an enormous bloody Rubens. The front windows overlooked the Court Theatre, where Osborne and the other Angry Young Men, who were his generation, had found their audience.

Another Canadian who seemed to be settled in permanently, and who was a friend of many of the others I mentioned, was Anne McDermid, a native Torontonian who had been in Paris during the 1968 riots but was now launched on a long career as a literary agent in London (not to return to Canada until the mid-1990s). Her office, in a Soho back street, stood at the top of a staircase beside which ran, under several generations of grime, an extraordinary eighteenth-century mural. Anne was full of ebullient charm and quick wit and had surprising connections. She had met Leonard Woolf, for example, and she chaperoned Samuel Beckett whenever he tiptoed across the Channel and out of exile. "He's not the troublesome sort of author," Anne would say cheerfully. "I find that I can stick him in a strip club in the morning on my way to the office and he'll sit there quite happily until I arrive to pick him up at the end of the day."

There being so many wires back to Canada, then, I'm hard pressed to explain why I was apparently representing Can lit in the Commonwealth context that evening at the Book League, but I too fulfilled everyone's low expectations: an odd, awkward figure, hesitant of speech and clumsy in gesture, with hair I had to keep brushing out of my eyes. (But at least I wasn't so boring or insecure as the New Zealander, whoever he or she was.)

As our performances deteriorated, the master of ceremonies (and now the Poet Laureate), Ted Hughes, a sullen and frightening figure, wearing a brown leather coat that matched his brown leather hair, became even less communicative than normal. The head of the League, desperate for chat topics, was obviously trying to think of a Canadian, any Canadian, after whose robust health he could inquire. At length he asked me to remember him to his old and dear friend Ned Pratt. It was my sad duty to tell him that E.J. Pratt had passed away in 1964, struck down in mid-career at the age of eighty or ninety.

The National Book League was a useful place because membership was only a few pounds and included use of its facilities in Albemarle Street, which runs off Piccadilly, parallel to Old Bond Street, an area of the West End that would have been too expensive to set foot in otherwise. Using the League's subsidized salon bar as a meeting place, and its library as a work area, gave me access to a whole sector of London that I wouldn't have known. The only drawback was that it had no residential accommodation, unlike, say, the Commonwealth [now Royal Overseas] League, which occupied two large eighteenth-century houses knocked together at the end of St James's Place, a cul-de-sac off the upper end of St James's, and was thus prohibitive, at least to me.

By a strange coincidence, my future spouse, whom I hadn't yet met at the time, was working near by, at one of the posh hotels in Park Lane. She had been employed in Toronto by the locally owned Four Seasons group, which now extended to the Inn on the Park: the only Canadian-owned hotel in London and thus one that drew a disproportionate share of the high-end Canadian custom. Janet Inksetter, as she then was, had been working behind the scenes until one day when Lester Pearson appeared at the desk, carrying his own garment bag and asking for his room, which no one on duty could find a record of, because they didn't know who he was. Janet straightened out the mix-up and made the management realize that the hotel needed a Canadian to handle public relations. Thus she was working and even living in swank surroundings, existing in the milieu of country weekends and the like, while I lived in a Dickensian slum in the City, panning for the exiguous living I have described. Yet the fact that we were often in close enough proximity to have met, if fate had acted differently, only reinforces, I believe, the point I was making earlier about the essential mobility, physically and hence socially as well, of people in London at that time. With a little bit of knowledge, which could be acquired mostly by covert research and close observation, one could live quite well in London, even if officially poor.

In those days, it was not even expensive to pop over to Paris to hang out at such places as George

Whitman's Shakespeare & Company, the English-language bookshop that claimed direct descent from Sylvia Beach's but was in a different location, near Notre Dame. George (who must make brief appearances in scores of published memoirs) was often reluctant to sell his books but was always willing to put up visiting writers in the guest room set aside for that purpose. He was a big favourite of the Beats, who wished desperately to believe his periodic assertion that he was a descendant of Walt Whitman (for Canadians, he would kindly claim to be from Saskatoon).

I was accustomed to keeping the assorted parts of my life tightly compartmentalized. In Toronto, as before, I felt I had to ensure that each set of acquaintances remained ignorant of the existence of all the others. But London was so much bigger and more complicated a molecular structure that I could achieve my goal by the simple expedient of urban geography. Journalists I petitioned for hand-outs were mostly to be found along the eastbound route through Fleet Street that I showed to Dan Williman two decades later. A short westward stroll took me to the reading room of the British Museum, where I could pick out some of the regulars, such as the elfish figure of Vincent Brome, biographer and novelist, whose memoir *Confessions of a Writer* is one of the most accurate depictions I know of the writing life. Many of the book publishers were also to be found in Bloomsbury. Their physical premises were often surprisingly small. For example, André Deutsch, a promising firm of the day, seemed to occupy the space of a good-sized bedsit; but then I was also astonished to see the inside of the *Times Literary Supplement* and realize that the paper was put out every week by a staff of, I believe, three. Then a little farther still and I was in the separate and exclusive world around the Park, where by rights I didn't belong but where I had worked out elaborate rituals of existence and honed my skills (akin to alchemy or locksmithing) at living well without capital or even an income. At the London Library in St James's Square, for example, one could wangle visiting student's privileges and read elephantine bound volumes of *The Times* back to 1785 while perched precariously atop one of the rickety wooden ladders in the cellar. Similarly, there was (still is, I believe) a health club in one of the office buildings on the east side of St James's Street where foreigners were taken in as visiting members at almost no cost. It was there, eventually, while sitting naked in the sauna with two other fellows in their twenties, that I knew I should leave London.

I had seen the pair around the club, may even have known their names. With the steam rising from the sizzling rocks, they were discussing first the present dockers' strike (the first since 1928) and then an upcoming by-election. I wanted to join in, for I had strong views, clear opinions and fresh gossip on these very matters. But I hesitated, judging, correctly, that as soon as they heard the first of my transatlantic vowels, they might tolerate me for a few minutes out of politeness but would never permit me to be part of their conversation. This wasn't business, after all, it was a matter of camaraderie.

In London I felt more at home, culturally, than anywhere else, infinitely more so than I had in the States, but to those who had London as their birthright I was welcomed only as part of the passing spectacle, as part of a fashion. Canada was not always friendly either. "You've picked a difficult bunch of folks to try to live among," a friend from Madras said years later, with what I think was precise insight. "All these northern types, these Angles and Saxons and Teutons, all these Brits and Yanks and Canadians, they're a hard mob to warm up." In truth, I had never been anywhere (not at this writing, not on this planet) where I might be mistaken for a native. Perhaps no such place existed. That being the case, of course, I could only return to Canada, where there were (and are) many wandering souls like me. They never get close to the mechanical plant or other high-security areas, but then they're not often persecuted in any organized manner or even as individuals, so long as they don't exceed their station or try to pass. I would spend the rest of my twenties trying to learn just exactly what and how much I could get away with. A great deal, as it turns out, given the tolerance that was the other face of Canada's aloofness. In an imperfect universe, what could be fairer than that? As I got older, I tended to settle for the utopia at hand rather than the distant mirage. But at the time of which I am writing now, the honesty of my public utterances did not often reach the levels found in my private thoughts. After Vancouver, London is the city I love best. After Toronto and Vancouver, it's where I've spent the most time over the years and it's the place I have got to know best. But following this first of many assaults on London, in 1970, I found myself drawn by romantic entanglements, and other poverties, back to a Toronto that was, at that very instant, starting to fly apart in decay, a period of steep decline that was practically simultaneous with its golden age, in a way that St Augustine would have understood perfectly but was maybe less apparent to many of us at the time.

CHAPTER ONE

# A Seventies Trip

**T**HE WAR MEASURES ACT was still in effect when I landed at Dorval in Montreal. To be sure, the long excitement was nearly over, but not lingering seemed an essential part of prudent behaviour. Using a *nom de guerre*, I bought a train ticket through to Toronto but got off at Kingston and switched to a bus. Leaving the Toronto coach terminal at Bay and Edward, I went to the Ford Hotel, directly opposite, where I registered, under a second name.

In Toronto, of course, soldiers had not been in evidence as they had in Quebec. Indeed, I was told, the city seemed to go along quite normally. In theory, the declaration of emergency powers may have affected the entire country, but in practice the federal government was concerned only with sovereigntists in Quebec, hundreds of whom had been rounded up. Toronto's cops by comparison had merely used the events in the lower province as an excuse for harassing a small handful of known troublemakers. Still, it was best to be careful until the situation became clear. I lay low a few days at the Ford, a place long famous for its round-the-clock anonymity, then found a small apartment—an attic bachelorette—on Bernard Avenue not far from Avenue Road. Its cost was glaringly little considering its location in the more expensive eastern part of the Annex. My possessions, which I had crammed into an old steamer trunk for transport by ship, arrived in the country some time later. The contents included manuscripts and notebooks.

Not much of what I'd written in England was worth preserving, so I had kept very little. Mainly what I had left was a small collection of new poems, which I added to over that winter. They were in a wearier voice than those I'd written earlier. They also looked much different on the page, as I was trying to erase the difference between the short lyric and the prose poem. They were, I suppose, the reverse of prose poems in that they looked like poems but were actually prose. John Robert Colombo was, I believe, the only person with the perspicuity to see this, rising above the general chorus of damnation to quote an old dictum of Pound's about verse that is as well written as prose. He was being too kind. I was trying to meld the virtues of the two forms but ended up combining their least appealing aspects. The result was (for me anyway) a new genre, one in which I had no special ability and which wasn't especially well suited to my goals. I called the collection *Our Man in Utopia*. I shouldn't have published it, at least not with Macmillan of Canada, for as my first book with a large commercial publisher it seemed to eclipse my far more interesting small-press collections for years to come, negatively influencing people's view. Still, the *act* of publishing it was fun, for Macmillan, at St Martin's House at 70 Bond Street, the building erected by the great English publishing dynasty in 1905 as its base in the Dominion, was a splendidly endearing place. It was actually as close I ever got to the style of book publishing practised in Bloomsbury and elsewhere in central London.

Canadian memoirs of a certain period pay homage *en passant* to the talents of Hugh Eayrs, who had run Macmillan in its glory days of the 1920s and 1930s (and whose son, James Eayrs, a political scientist and Macmillan author, in my time wrote an excellent foreign-policy column for the *Star*). Hugh Eayrs's Macmillan was that of Hector Charlesworth's autobiographies, W.H. Blake's translation of Louis Hémon's *Maria Chapdelaine* and the general boom in high-quality Canadian trade books by writers such as E.J. Pratt and Mazo De la Roche. His successor, doted on in a slightly later generation of memoirs, was John Gray. When Gray's own memoirs appeared years afterwards, I observed in my journal: "Looking at the photographs in the book confirms my original impression: that he was a man who once bore a resemblance to the young Joseph Cotten (the Joseph Cotten of *Citizen Kane*) but that the two faces had diverged at some point in the 1950s." My other impression was that he didn't much care for my own looks.

Gwen MacEwen and Tom Marshall, both new Macmillan authors at the time, were urging me to see if the company would take on my ersatz poems.

When I turned up to keep the appointment, Gray came out of his office to greet me, took one look at my long hair, turned on his heels and scurried back inside.

"I think you'd be more comfortable with Mr Derry," he called back over his shoulder as he slammed the door.

His materializing, his disappearance, his redirecting me and his slamming were all in one smooth continuous motion, quite impressive in its way. At that point, Ramsay Derry stepped in to try to make up for his boss's rudeness and trundled me off to his own office, a modest cubicle in a long row of same, where an exhalation of editors turned out a large trade list, heavy in Canadian history, politics and literature. Ramsay, who would become a loyal friend to me and my work, was a youngish Canadian who had himself returned from Britain not long before. Prior to becoming an editor at Cambridge University Press, he had worked for Collins as an itinerant Bible salesman in the North Country. His inventory of samples had comprised a stunning variety of big Bibles and small, Old Testament alone or Old and New together, with or without the Apocrypha, and included even the seldom-seen Red Letter Edition, with all the words supposedly spoken by Christ printed in ink the colour of His blood. When sufficiently relaxed over lunch, Ramsay could still be persuaded to recreate some of his pedlar's spiel: "No, no, madam, not plastic—*leatheroid.*"

Ramsay was already the editor of such important Macmillan authors as the crusty old historian Donald Creighton. Soon he would fulfil the same function for Robertson Davies (who chose Dunstan Ramsay as the name of the main character in *Fifth Business*, his first Macmillan novel—Dunstan being close to Duncan, the name of Ramsay Derry's father, a prominent geologist). I always enjoyed visiting Ramsay in his office, through whose window you could just observe the tops of Eaton's and Simpsons at Queen and Yonge, a few blocks to the south and west.

The lobby of St Martin's House resembled a well-used rectory, with unswept marble steps and old oak wainscoting in need of an oiling. Off to the right as one entered was the so-called library, actually a sample room, where dusty specimen copies had been accumulating for years. At the end of the short corridor was a glass partition behind which sat the telephonist (that was her job title). Others to whom I've spoken have contradicted me in this, but in my own memory at least the telephonist wore a wig that more than often seemed to be listing to starboard, in a manner that called to mind contemporary descriptions of William Lyon Mackenzie (who spent his last years, 1849–61, in a rowhouse immediately next door, where, some claimed, his ornery republican ghost still wandered).

When the telephone rang, the telephonist would answer in her plummy and mellifluous voice before directing the call to its destination, selecting one strand from the tangled centipede of wires connected to the old switchboard and patching it into the proper socket. This she could accomplish only by squinting through her lorgnette. Even so, she often put callers through to the wrong extensions, sometimes with hilarious results, or else mistakenly terminated some important transatlantic conference that John Gray and Hugh Kane (the affable Irish gentleman-publisher, who had come to Macmillan from McClelland & Stewart) were having with, oh I don't know, Sir Stanley Unwin or another London notable of that sort.

The telephonist also controlled visitors' access to the upper floors. Waiting to catch her attention between mangled telephone calls, I would always glance up at the portrait engravings of Daniel Macmillan and bas-reliefs of late Macmillan of Canada authors such as Grey Owl. I would announce myself as G. Owl, calling on R. Derry. She would then ring upstairs and announce cheerily, "Mr Derry, there's a Mr Owl here to see you." She never caught on, so I never tired of the prank, nor did Ramsay, who would always be laughing when I stepped out of the lift.

Other eccentricities of Macmillan of Canada included the tea lady pushing her little trolley from floor to floor at the appropriate hour each afternoon. Actually, she was only the tea lady part time. Her other duties included visiting each editor's desk in the morning, before editorial business began, and hanging a fresh linen towel underneath, so that each person might have his own to carry to the loo. I use the masculine pronoun deliberately, for female editors, such as Ramsay's protégée Jane (later Saeko) Usukawa, were presumed to be immune from Nature's vulgar demands on the body and had to go through the day in a state of towellessness.

To be sure, such discrimination was a bit over the top even by the sexist standards of the 1970s. In most other ways, however, Macmillan's atmosphere was attractive. But the atmosphere, and the mandate that was inseparable from it, deteriorated steadily after the original owners, fearing an increase in political backlash, sold out and Macmillan was taken over by the first in an endless sequence of Canadian companies. Like the study of illiteracy and police corruption in Jamaica, the case of Macmillan of Canada is a classic instance of how infrastructure breaks down whenever the British withdraw. The decline, while slow, was steady, leading to the point that, by the late 1980s, after the veteran Linda McKnight stepped down as its publisher to become a literary agent, Macmillan of Canada, as it still continued to call itself, would be in the enviable position of never producing a worthwhile book except by accident. I can only hope this will change one day.

I was scribbling quite madly all this while, supporting myself with whatever hack work there was to be had. This extended far beyond reviewing and editing into the realm of the sub-literary and the blessedly anonymous. For example, I once researched and wrote the captions, hundreds of them in all, for some large art book, and was one of the uncredited authors of a guide to Toronto restaurants (or was it a guide to historic architecture?—I've forgotten; the note of detached gushing is the same in both cases). For about a year, I strove for wit and learning in the introductions to classic Hollywood films of the 1930s and 1940s that I wrote for a staff announcer to read on CBC television. This was by no means a lifestyle I monopolized. One of the prolific art critics of those days made a subsistence living writing the gentle verbal nonsense supposedly spoken *ad libitum* by the all-night disc jockeys at the city's principal FM station. It was a task that called for the strictest attention to the difference in tone and timbre, so rigidly enforced in those days, between FM and AM jocks. Another critic of the time supplemented her income by occasional bouts of—*prostitution* doesn't seem the correct term in this case. She would visit well-off gentlemen in their homes or offices and, using her belt, pretend to whip their asses. This activity was never alluded to in dust-jacket copy.

As my place on Bernard was barely big enough to live in when the hide-a-bed was extended full length, I rented a cheap work space overlooking Yonge Street, in the Edwardian post office at the corner of Charles. The ground floor was a cinema, Cinecity, Toronto's most important and longest running art house, where one saw everything, speaking alphabetically, from Costa-Gavras to Warhol but not forgetting Fellini and Godard. The upper floors were home to the pioneer gay-rights organization CHAT, the Community Homophile Association of Toronto, as well as to several bizarre business enterprises. One of these was a magazine called *Jewish Dialog*. Its premises looked like some old Bay Street boiler room, virtually bare except for many battered desks where a large and constantly changing band of high-pressure salespeople sat working the phones, selling advertising to every Jewish-owned business they could identify from the Yellow Pages. The magazine needed *some* editorial content to keep the ads from running together in a blur, and this was supplied by Joe Rosenblatt, the poet, who solicited verse, fiction and reviews.

My own one-room office, with frosted glass in the front, was immediately next door. There I carried out all my nefarious enterprises. For a time these included a literary underground newspaper that I put out with my multi-talented friend Joe Nickell. Its contents puzzled people. One commentator appeared to speak for the majority when he wrote with some disbelief that our publication seemed to be a cross between *Guerrilla* and *Queen's Quarterly*. The former was an anarchist paper of the day, edited by Jim Christy and designed by Robert MacDonald. We once published an essay by Jim purporting to prove that B. Traven, the mysterious German who wrote *The Treasure of the Sierra Madre*, was actually Artur Cravan, the Zurich-born poet, boxer, putative nephew of Oscar Wilde and self-proclaimed deserter from seventeen different armies, who had disappeared about 1920. I suggested a follow-up piece proving that Traven in turn was really Frederick Philip Grove.

Another regular contributor to the paper was a poet who lived in a big dirty old bow-windowed house on the east side of Spadina Road, about midway between Bloor and Dupont. One day he told me that the apartment below his had come up for rent and said he hoped I would take it. I did. Or, rather, typically for me in those days, I moved some of my stuff there while finishing out the lease on Bernard, so that for a while I had two cheap little places instead of a single decent one: two cheap little places but very different from each other, thus facilitating the continuance of parallel lives, the professional and the personal, the public and the private, the journalistic and the literary. For much of 1971 my compass had only three points. There was the house on Bernard, where most of my possessions from England still lay unpacked. There was the one on Spadina Road ("a hovel," the *Star* once called it, a little unkindly, I thought) furnished with pieces of broken and cast-off furniture. And there was the office at Yonge and Charles, where, melodramatically to say the least, we kept a bottle of gasoline atop the file cabinet so that the records could be destroyed in an instant should the imagined danger of a raid by some authority or other ever prove to be more than just faddish paranoia.

At about this time a vacancy occurred at Charles Street as well, but was quickly filled. A group of people from the likable clan of Canadian book publishing had come together to start the magazine *Books in Canada* in one of the offices above me on the top floor. I had a piece in the first issue and have continued to write for it over the years, with long interruptions. The founding group included Val Clery, an Irishman who had made the unlikely transition from British commando in the Second World War to CBC Radio producer and eventually became the saloon critic of the *Star*; the droopy-eyed Douglas Marshall, then a member of the editorial staff at *Maclean's;* Jack Jensen, from Denmark, a popular bachelor round town who was chief remainder buyer for the Coles bookstore chain and lived a few doors away; Mary Lu Toms, a friend of Jensen's; and Randall Ware, whom I'd first known when he was a bookstore clerk in the late sixties and who would go on to many different positions in the publishing bureaucracy in Toronto and in Ottawa. These brief descriptions are probably enough to show the variegated yet strangely coherent nature of the organization. I add only that Clery, who wrote well himself and lived with the editor of the publishing trade journal *Quill & Quire* and then with her successor in that job, was *Books in Canada*'s first editor. I won't comment on the quality of product, for Clery in particular has always been pugnacious in defence of the work they did. I'll say only that these were not particularly bookish people (I suspected one of them of actually having the reading skills of a child). Yet in the early years the magazine did maintain a distinctive charm, part amateurism (in the best sense of the word), part literary voyeurism. There was even a circle of visiting writers to admire. One was Al Purdy, who would come into the city from Ameliasburg from time to time and put up in a sleazy hotel on Jarvis Street. Another was the litigious Earle Birney, who would stay at Jensen's. It was while departing Jensen's in a taxi for the airport that Earle was injured in a collision with another taxi from the same fleet: a lawyer's dream come true.

*Books in Canada* never had much money (in fact, the editor's job was a part-time one until 1990, when Paul Stuewe assumed the post), and in the early days at least there was a role for some kind of volunteer or unpaid apprentice. The first one of these was a woman who, I hoped, would fill the hole in my life. It may seem odd to divide one's life into segments this way, according to the relationships one has had. But what other kind of calendar than this, based on the deepest internal emotions rather than external events artificially imposed, could possibly have more logic? In any case, Rachel Glazer was a Montrealer who had a degree in English from McGill and had a little time on her hands now that she was living in Toronto, where she had originally come to teach. I would find excuses to nip upstairs to the *Books in Canada* office, and we would slip out for coffee and later for lunches. She had an interesting family (her brother had been the first nude actor in Great Britain after the Lord Chamberlain's Office struck down the old censorship rules), and she was interested in being part of what seemed the still new or at least revitalized and re-energized world of Can lit, feeling that her university studies had kept its existence secret from her more or less. She had great charm and grace, and a number of my friends—for example, Ramsay Derry—would become very fond of her. I'm not sure what she saw in me. Whatever it was, it was soon enough worn down by the incessant grinding action of reality. Looking back now, I see this pattern in my life: attraction to (as who would not be attracted to?) strong-willed, fiercely independent women with talent and sharp intelligence who, as they've grown even more so in the friendly environment I've tried to make for their abilities, have sometimes found me unable to keep up with their rapid rate of progress. Always the usher, never the bridegroom.

So it was that Rachel, too, set about changing her circumstances. On the strength of her degrees and new literary interests, she quickly found an editorial job at one of the American branch-plant publishers, the sort of operation that is forever taking a flyer in Canadian trade books, then quickly retreating back into the educational field when the market sends a message that the firm has no understanding of the native culture. It was the type of job that one could make interesting so long as one disguised the true quality of what one did. By publishing their work under one pretext or another, Rachel quickly got to know many Canadian writers and literary academics (one of whom became fixated on her and would telephone at all hours of the night with his unfulfilled erotic longings). Her sweatshop colleagues included a young woman from Paris who in her spare time was making new French translations of William Carlos Williams. Struggling to improve her limited grasp of strictly informal English, she once asked Rachel, "What is the meaning of this verb *to fuck*?" Another co-worker was an Eastern European feminist organizer married to the superrealist painter Jeremy Smith and living with him in a second-storey flat on Howland Avenue in the Annex. When the ground-floor equivalent directly across the street came available, Rachel grabbed it, and we moved in together, lining the long front corridor with bookshelves and punctuating our studious and culture-rich life with wild and ambitious parties.

Howland was an interesting street, its neat rows of late Victorian houses sometimes single-family homes, sometimes flats, sometimes communes. A block down lived one of Rachel's friends, a socialist agitator who was Earle Birney's mistress. In a previous life, in England, she had been Ian Fleming's secretary at *The*

*Sunday Times.* Fleming was so terrified of women, she remembered, that he could barely speak if any of them except her entered his office (why does this fail to surprise?). Another near neighbour was Jim Christy, who was now living with a former art student who shared his interests in anarchism, jazz and Blaise Cendrars, though their relationship was distinguished by extremes of agreement and discord. In the latter mode, she once started to destroy all his unpublished manuscripts after he'd stormed out of an argument. On another occasion, she rang Rachel and me late at night looking for $100 with which to go Jim's bail. I remember Rachel on the phone, dealing with the situation helpfully and efficiently, while I remained in bed, shouting over her shoulder for the ultimate amusement of my friend Jim, "A hundred bucks! What did he do, shoot E. Tupper Bigelow?"

Judge Bigelow was a luminary of the bench who had sent a number of our acquaintances up the proverbial river. I loved the names of the Toronto authorities one constantly found in the newspapers in those days. There was O.J. Silverthorne, for example, who was Ontario's film censor, and the ubiquitous H.B. Cottnam, the chief coroner, who seemed destined to get round to all of us eventually.

————————

One night in 1970 the CBC taped a marathon poetry reading at the old Gay Cinema on Parliament Street, which recently had been reclaimed as a radio studio. The occasion would live on in the memory of most of those present because Louis Dudek, that apostle of high culture, used a form of the verb *to fuck* that went out on the air. I can still see Robert Weaver, the CBC's producer of literary programmes, up in the control booth to the right of the stage, wincing a bit and suddenly puffing his pipe with unusual vigour. The whole story is told with great wit in Robin Skelton's autobiography, *Memoirs of a Literary Blockhead*, and it would be foolish of me to attempt to match his flair. Instead, I'll remember another incident that took place at the same event: my first meeting with Hugh Garner, a writer whose sensibility came out of the 1930s and 1940s but whose career, many will be surprised to remember, reached its all-too-brief zenith in the 1970s.

I remember walking along Queen Street in early spring 1968 and spotting the newly published, unexpurgated edition of his novel *Cabbagetown* in the display window of the Ryerson Press building (later the home of CITY-TV and MuchMusic). I'd admired the sure-footedness and old-fashioned integrity of a number of his stories, particularly the ones in *Men and Women*, but had never read the novel that even then dominated his reputation, for at that time I had not seen the twenty-year-old paperback. Reading the new edition a week later in Montreal, I remember thinking that it had more precision and less expansive garrulousness than I'd expected to find in so celebrated a piece of Depression social realism. It was obviously distilled from a lot of remembered experience, and was a marvellous picture of a lost Toronto growing up in spite of itself. Later I learned this last element was somewhat accidental. A journalistic type of fiction-writer, Garner as a fiction-writer was not much of a journalist, for when his recollections were used up, he had a terrible time with details arising from research. He was, I believe, the kind of creator who recalls rather than imagines or is spurred on by other people's work (Proust and Kerouac are the high and low examples).

A case in point is connected to my accidental meeting with him. I was standing at the back of the studio, behind the audience, when I recognized him from his jacket photographs: a fierce-looking almost tubby man on short legs, like an old Victorian chair that had lost some of its stuffing in the Salvation Army. He was in baggy trousers and an old tweed coat. As early pictures subsequently confirmed, he had once been a handsome fellow, but good looks had now given way to character, though his face, I think, had not then acquired all the rugosity that would distinguish it later.

Friends had warned me of his fearsome reputation as a battler with editors and public alike. I'd been fed horror stories of his barging into publishing houses demanding to see the president or toddling into small-claims court to file papers against this or that magazine when a cheque was slightly overdue. All these tales, combined with Garner's determinedly non-literary standing, let me know he was probably the last person one would expect to see at a poetry reading.

"I saw something about this in the paper," he said. His voice had been described variously as sounding like gears being stripped or like No. 30 sandpaper come to life. It now matched everyone's imitations of it.

"I just thought I'd come down and take a gander. I don't know much about this stuff."

We chatted awhile after the reading broke up. His mood made it clear that he considered the evening wasted.

In 1975 I discovered that he had remembered the building and its weird atmosphere and used them in *The Intruders*. To my knowledge he did not keep a journal or a general notebook, but instead carried around such impressions in his head until memory had done the necessary editing work. Now when I dip into his books I keep stumbling on details like that, which he worked smoothly into whatever piece of writing he had under way. In one story, the ambience of the old Savarin on Bay Street, a hang-out for people who worked on the *Telegram* in the days, brief as they were, when Garner wrote a column in the paper, is captured exactly (or much more so, I believe, than in Gwen MacEwen's poem about the same place). Another story makes me remember the precise way that lower York Street, now razed, used to feel. The list must be almost endless for people older than I am. When everyone who could have known them firsthand is dead, Garner's descriptions of spaces and types will add up to something like a tiny social history of his own time and place. Of course, he'll have to be rediscovered first. This may take a while, because in his last years Garner wore his reputation right down to the gums.

Not long after the Parliament Street encounter we had lunch together and that led to other lunches, from which my memory has salvaged a few conversational snippets. Garner had served in the Abraham

Lincoln Brigade in the Spanish Civil War, joining before the Mac-Paps were mustered in Canada, and he told me once that his great aim was to outlive "that sonofabitch Generalissimo Franco" (which he did, by a comfortable margin). But then he recanted in advance in case I wanted to quote him: not out of sheepishness but out of a strange love of trivial decorum, so at odds with the rest of his personality. I also remember his telling me, when he was adapting one of his stories for television, how the producer had gone over his draft and explained to him why the videotape medium made it impossible to shoot some of the exteriors he had written (one, I believe, involved a car plunging over a cliff). He was grateful for the advice (for once in his life) and was childlike with curiosity about the new technology. I also gleaned the fact that old friends of the public house sort called him Hughie, but though he would repeat the cognomen when recounting their conversations, he resented its use by others.

As we began seeing each other fairly often, I got a sense that he was in a rut in his career (which he'd talk about freely) if not in his actual creative life (which he'd never discuss with anyone, not even his oldest book-world friend, Bob Weaver).

I suspect he had had as many disappointments as triumphs. He was always proud of having had a story picked up for Martha Foley's *Best American Short Stories of 1952*, a feat never repeated in other years. But then when his son (who grew up to look just like him) and his daughter were small, he'd turned his attention to journalism and didn't publish any books between

1952 and 1962. When he finally brought out <u>*Silence on the Shore*</u>, there were acrimonious words between him and Jack McClelland. A stevedores' strike or some similar action had left the bound books, which had been manufactured in the UK, sitting on the docks in Montreal. Weeks passed. Garner felt the lost momentum seriously hurt the book's sales and reception, and he may have been right. Certainly it's his most artistically satisfying long piece of fiction, the one into which he put all the effort he was capable of, but it never helped him to overcome the dominance of the inferior *Cabbagetown* and to show people a better <u>Garner</u> than the one they knew. The character of Grace, the German landlady, was one of the most fully developed and most memorable female characters in Canadian fiction of the day, almost on the same level as Margaret Laurence's Hagar in her interior life; but then it is one of the unaccepted truths that Garner's most completely realized characters are the women of his generation (think of the schoolteachers in *Violation of the Virgins*), though if one made that statement out loud, people of younger generations would laugh. Anyway, Garner swore, as he frequently did when relations got rough, that he'd never publish another book with M&S. Jack McClelland must have replied in kind. Both were true to their word. The sorrow is that after *Silence on the Shore*, Garner never really put his whole self into a book again, or so I have come to believe.

Which is not to say that he was unproductive. When I first met him, he was in his late fifties and resembled nothing so much as an old hound whose ears others dogs had chewed on in various arguments about nothing in particular. Given that, it was surprising that he was so obviously at the beginning of a remarkable burst of energy that would take him through most of the 1970s. He was, however, having trouble finding a publisher after the murder of Ryerson Press, partly because he was always willing to make do with as hastily written a manuscript as his editor of the moment would accept. He had a detective thriller this time (if I recall correctly, not yet called *The Sin Sniper*) and was obviously getting turned down left and right. When he had exhausted all the commercial houses, I volunteered to try to place it with a small press. Naturally I was rebuffed, as I knew I would be, and mocked for imagining in my wildest fantasies that such a connection was possible. Eventually, Garner sold it to Pocket Books of Canada, as the Simon & Schuster branch plant then styled itself. The company began putting all his old books back into print, eventually giving him the ultimate accolade of his own point-of-sale display cartons—and making him, I suppose, most of the money he lived on in his last seven or eight years. (Alas, he never got to see the movie version of *The Sin Sniper*, renamed *Stone Cold Dead*, but I'm sure he had already sold the film rights before he died.) One of the people at Pocket Books was a rough diamond who was passionately interested in horse-racing and the like. Garner and he got along fine.

The above story isn't to suggest that Garner was incapable of taking rejection with equanimity. He had so suspicious and quarrelsome an attitude towards publishers that it spilled over into a kind of insouciance ("I've seen 'em come and I've seen 'em go," he would say after every severing of relations). He was a working stiff in a middle-class world who never acquired much of the polish one needs to get by, chose not to perhaps. Yet this very fact meant that he showed, on a rudimentary level, almost Old World manners one seldom sees expressed so genuinely in people who've forgotten where they come from.

If he rang when I happened to be out ("Just wanted to yak," he'd growl), Rachel would invariably remark afterwards on his telephone deportment, which was almost courtly. As far as I could tell, this was an attitude he reserved for women. When I'd return the call, he would immediately begin unreeling his remarkably scatological vocabulary in story after story, pausing frequently for a hacking cough so chronic that it became a kind of subverbal punctuation.

One morning I ran into him at the CBC accounting department, above Bassel's Restaurant at Yonge and Gerrard, where he'd come to sign a contract for one of the many short stories of his that Weaver bought for his programme, *Anthology*. He was more dressed up than I'd ever seen him, with a starched shirt and a proper suit and tie, both of recent vintage and obviously not inexpensive. Afterwards we walked to the Honey Dew on Carlton for a coffee. He'd just undergone a prostate operation, he said, and wasn't able to consume any alcohol for a while. The thought clearly depressed him, but he was in good form otherwise. I asked offhandedly what he was doing downtown so early when he was usually working at home. I supposed that he was turned out for some important meeting. But no, he got decked out, as he would have phrased it, simply to put his name on a form. There was no question but that this was what you did when you were reared in the fish-and-chippers' Cabbagetown of the 1920s. You kept the place spotless, always had curtains on the windows, read the *Evening Telegram* in preference to the bolshevik *Daily Star*— and always dressed when you went to business or otherwise had truck with people better off than yourself.

Even in his frequently outrageous moments there was a politeness underneath: he could call someone a goddam cocksucking lying sonofabitch more casually, and with less real rancour, and so more oblique affection, than anyone else I've ever known. The real nastiness, which lurked beneath his skin like an itch, usually came only after he'd had more than a good deal to drink. It seemed to surface as though in anticipation of the tragedy that usually followed such bouts.

*Maclean's* once called him Canada's best-known drunk since Sir John A. Macdonald, and he would always discuss his problem freely when called on to do so, though later it became clear that this was to keep from having to mention less obvious but even more painful topics. Until the last couple of years of his life he was a binge drinker. "I never drink when I'm working on a book," he would say proudly. Once finished, however, he made up for lost time. The bouts would last days, weeks, even a month or more it was said, and leave a sketchy trail of altercations and illness. I remember being told in detail about an incident he relates in his memoir, *One Damn Thing after Another* (a book that seems to me to represent the wholesale loss of his powers and his judgement towards the end). The story concerns a bill for breakage at the Chateau Laurier in Ottawa. The doorman saw him weaving dangerously and said something to the effect of, "Go sleep it off, buddy," whereupon Garner knocked him through the glass panels of the revolving door. Despite his short stature, he remained a tough fellow well beyond middle age.

Stories about his ugliness when drunk in public places are legion among people who found themselves with him in lifts and on planes. I'd never actually seen him swacked until I went to the launching of one of his books. He took the need to celebrate rather more seriously than did the reviewers in attendance, and ended up pitching to and fro on the balls of his feet, vocally dividing the guests, according to gender, into prickfaces and whores. Rachel and I invited him to one of our parties, and he arrived early and with his old-fashioned manners at their brightest. I immediately sensed our mistake in asking him to a party where everyone else was younger by at least a generation, but whatever discomfort he felt only made him unwind more earnestly. Rachel offered him wine and poured a respectable dollop.

"Jesus Christ Almighty, you can do better than that for godsakes. There's not enough there to make an IODE member blush."

Garner was the last to leave. I learned later that he got mugged on the way home.

There followed, in good order, one of his drying-out spells at a place called Homewood in Guelph.

While taking the cure he would go through the motions of therapy by participating in crafts classes. Ceramic ashtrays were his specialty and he would pass them out to guests at his apartment. On the bottoms of them he would scratch his name in block letters with a knife: an artisan but with an artist's pride, and vice versa. In giving me one of these objects once, he complained that Homewood, formerly a private clinic, had recently been taken over by the province. "I used to hobnob with cabinet ministers, big businessmen, that kind of guy. Now all that's changed. We used to get a better class of drunk there, you know what I mean? Not all this riff-raff." He laughed a laugh that showed his gold tooth and his bridgework.

My worst encounter with Garner on booze came shortly after he published his pitiful autobiography. A producer from the CBC programme *Take Thirty* phoned to say he had this great idea—interviewing Garner *in situ* in Cabbagetown. I suppressed ennui, for taking Garner back to Cabbagetown was among the striking journalistic clichés of the period, like stories on the Oak Island treasure. The producer wanted to film him in a pub talking to younger writers. He thought I might be one. Did I know a young female writer who would participate? I suggested my friend Nancy Naglin (about whom more later), because I suspected she could use her $50 fee as much as I could use mine. On the appointed day, she and I drove to a beer parlour far out on Gerrard Street East, where a mobile unit had already strewn cables about the area. It was noon. The plan was to film the two of us, Garner and the host of the show, Paul Soles, for an hour, in order to allow for an edited-down ten- or fifteen-minute segment.

As soon as I entered, I saw Garner across the room and knew we were in trouble. He was weaving noticeably and backslapping strangers preparatory to the kill. At closer range I could see that his pupils were dilated. When he had been made up and miked he turned out to be in even worse condition than I'd supposed. I was placed at one end of a Formica-topped table with Garner on the other side, flanked by Nancy and by Soles. The director threw a signal, but before Soles could ask a question, Garner, staring at Soles and at Nancy, blurted out in a hoarse stage whisper audible throughout the room, "Jesus H. Christ, I'm surrounded by a couple o' Jews!" From that point on, it was downhill; a friend in the crew told me that I unconsciously made a little palisade of all the salt shakers and vinegar bottles and tried to hide behind it. The few Jews who occur in Garner's fiction are admirable, almost noble, and I believe they are a reflection of Garner's identification with victims of persecution. But then the best of Garner seemed to come out only in his fiction. The day-to-day Garner was full of the crude working-class prejudices of his generation.

At the next table a pair of old fellows with Legion pins began to make off-camera remarks about Garner's apparent flirtation with show business, and he excused himself several times to go over and threaten violence. At another point he slammed his lapel-mike down on the hard table, causing the sound technician some grief. Paul Soles bore up with professionalism and grace, but after about fifteen minutes the director called a halt and the crew began to pack up. All the while, Garner, a chain-smoker, had been gesticulating wildly with a lighted cigarette. Once Nancy and I were outside, she told me that he had unwittingly brought it to rest against her trouser leg. There was a hole in her corduroys about the size of a sixpence with a corresponding burn beneath. I asked her why she hadn't cried out in pain.

"I didn't want to call his attention to it," she said, "lest the smell of burning flesh excite him further."

After that I didn't hear from him for what seemed a long time and was reluctant to renew the contact, given his anti-Semitic outburst. But then one afternoon he picked up the telephone—an act, I knew, that was itself an unstated apology to all concerned, though his ostensible reason in calling was to tell me the rest of the story. It seemed he had lingered at the pub long after we and the TV unit had left. Departing at last, and in an even worse state than when we had arrived, he hailed a taxi to go to his apartment on Erskine Avenue, just north of Eglinton, off Yonge. He told the driver to stop on the way at the Summerhill liquor store. It was a blizzardy day, and when Garner emerged on the icy pavement with bottles crooked in both arms, the driver thoughtfully whipped round to the passenger side to open the door for him. A tactical mistake, for Garner interpreted this as a slur on his condition and began heckling the driver once they were under way again. At one point, they exchanged particularly harsh words and Garner slugged the man across the back of the head. The driver announced that he was taking them to the cop shop, where he intended to file a complaint. Whereupon Garner, with the incisive logic that sometimes accompanies inebriation, replied that, since he wasn't being taken home as requested, he certainly had no intention of paying the fare. When they arrived at No. 53 Division at Yonge and Montgomery, Garner was thrown into a holding cell for the night.

"A couple of young Scottish cops worked me over pretty good," he told me. "I've been feeling kind of punk. That's why I haven't called."

He was well past sixty at the time, still to outward appearances astoundingly resilient to physical abuse but beginning to assume perhaps a slightly more *laissez-faire* attitude towards his fellow humans. He bore the police no particular grudge. They were simply part of the way things were. He imagined that other people should look on him with similar generosity, though whether they did so was a question for which, to use a Garnerism, he didn't give a tinker's dam.

———

Kildare Dobbs, who wrote beautifully, was an Irish Protestant of ancient lineage. Indeed, there was actually an ancestral castle in some remote part of Ireland. It had fallen into extreme disrepair, however, and one of Kildare's distant relatives, in an effort to pay the tax arrears, had leased out the chapel, in which W.B. Yeats once prayed, to a California-based cult that worshipped Isis. "They've painted an enormous mural of a vagina behind the altar," Kildare said appreciatively. He was round and pink-skinned, with wisps of white hair, a wry smile and a low mumbly voice that forced his interlocutors to lean into every conversation at an angle of about thirty degrees.

His background was fetchingly implausible but nonetheless authentic. He had been born in India, where his father was a district commissioner in the colonial civil service, and he could remember that in his childhood a parade of elephants had been sum-moned to entertain at one of his birthday parties. Despite his start in life (and despite being, like Val Clery, a neutral Irish national), he had enlisted in the Royal Navy during the war as an ordinary seaman. Only afterwards did he go to Cambridge. He had come to Canada in the 1950s following his own stint in the colonial system as a district officer in East Africa. This part of his past was the subject of recurrent rumour. As far as I could tell, from bits and pieces Kildare told me over the years, he had befriended many Africans, thereby violating the social taboos of the British. When one of his African friends was charged with ivory theft and looked to be sent down for a long stretch, Kildare took the rap for him, knowing that as a European he would receive only a light sentence. One of the other whites in his cell-block, he told me, used to berate their African guards loudly for leaving the door open. "If you stupid bastards don't lock the cell behind me," the man used to say, "anybody could walk in here while I'm asleep and make off with my kit."

It was typical of Kildare that he would see the humour in prison life, or pretend to. In fact, though,

I'm sure his African experience had hurt him deeply. For years, I believe, even when he had worked as an editor at Macmillan in Bond Street, he had been trying to turn the trauma into a novel. He had had several grants but could never quite seem to finish (and indeed the book was not published until 1981, and then in short form, as the title piece of *Pride and Fall: A Novella and Six Stories*, only to disappear under a withering review in the *Globe* by a young postmodernist who had declared a personal war against realism).

When I got to know him, Kildare had switched jobs with Bob Fulford—Fulford going from a book column at the *Star* to *Saturday Night* and Kildare from *Saturday Night* to a book column at the *Star*. Kildare had an assistant about my own age who did much of the hard work on the book page. This was Marni Jackson, in later years an important non-fiction writer (and, alas, someone who, as she finally confessed to me one day, avoided me because I inadvertently reminded her of the fact that she had stuttered as a child—a brave observation for her to make and one for which I've admired her ever since). Kildare himself stuck pretty close to the task of writing a column for Saturday and two others during the week. His prose was fluent, facile and witty, far more pleasurable to read than that of anyone else on the paper, but he didn't recognize the publishing world's consensual agreement as to what was important. He went his own eccentric way, using some very offbeat books indeed, Irish ones in particular, as the points of departure for his miniature essays. In 1963, when the Governor-General's Award for Non-fiction was still a literary award rather than one for journalism, Kildare had won for his wonderfully graceful book of autobiographical sketches, *Running to Paradise*. Hugh Garner was so outraged at this example of *belles lettres* (Garner could imbue the French language with enormous contempt) that he'd told a radio audience, "Anybody who would give an award to a nicey-nursey, namby-pamby book like that would give an award"—and here he searched for just the perfect insult—"*to a book about cats.*"

Despite this unsolicited guidance from Garner, the *Star*'s management, I think, never knew quite what to make of Kildare. They didn't know what a gem they had. Once, I remember, the entertainment editor, acting out of cruelty or incompetence, thought it would be fun to take Kildare off books for a day and send him to Hamilton to interview Liberace, who had brought his piano and his outrageously campy costumes to Hamilton Place. Kildare returned in the afternoon with a splendid interview. It began with some untranslated Latin verses (albeit ones by the always accessible Catullus, not by Martial, say, or Tibullus—even Kildare recognized that this was the populist *Star* and not the *Globe and Mail*). After that, the entertainment editor left him alone. Or would have done so if he himself had been left alone, which he wasn't. He was constantly getting rockets from above, some of which he would try to pass off to Kildare and other members of his staff before getting burned.

In the early 1970s, the *Star* was run like a gladiatorial spectacle. I say this without any attempt at provocation. The publisher, Beland Honderich, had his heir apparent in an editor named Martin Goodman, a rough-and-tumble newsroom executive, a proud philistine but obviously very bright, who chewed gum and never seemed to sleep. To keep Goodman on his toes, the publisher brought in a steady succession of hotshot potential rivals. He brought them in at great expense from Fleet Street, from big American news organizations and of course from every other important publication in Canada. Each would spend a year or two working twenty hours a day in an attempt to bump Goodman off his perch. Goodman, still chewing gum, would simply work twenty-four. This style of management made life difficult for everyone below the top-most echelon. People used to twist an old proverb to suit an immediate need: "I had no shoes and felt sorry for myself until I met a man who worked at the *Star*." Goodman, poor soul, died of cancer at an early age, before he could don the mantle he'd worked so hard to keep others from ever wearing.

As Kildare wasn't interested in Canadian publishing *per se*, I was pretty much free to choose the new Canadian books I wanted to comment on. I did a lot of enjoyable lunching with him as well. Whichever restaurant he decided to patronize seemed to honour him with his own permanent table, which would then evolve into a kind of salon. At this time he favoured a phoney Irish place on Adelaide, phoney because it was owned by a Greek who would always make a point of saying, in his thick Greek accent, that he hailed from County Sparta. Kildare and he would then engage in lovely banter about the Old Country.

Kildare had some appealing antiquarian interests.

He and I were the only people either of us knew who had read the American decadent writer Edgar Saltus, author of such novels as *Imperial Purple* (1892) and *The Imperial Orgy* (1920). Kildare liked him for the sheer metaphoric awfulness of his prose, which he could quote by the yard for cautionary effect, whereas I, still in my early twenties, took the symbolist and decadent manner quite seriously, as with James Gibbons Huneker's *Painted Veils*, Remy de Gourmont's *A Night in the Luxembourg* or, more famously, J.-K. Huysmans's *A rebours* (immune, it shames me to realize now, to its virulent misogyny). Kildare was tolerant of my enthusiasms. For my part, I listened with fascination when he told me of his desire (never realized) to produce a fully annotated historical edition of the *Book of Common Prayer*.

At the beginning of the decade, the *Star* abandoned its old Gothic skyscraper on King for a new building at One Yonge Street, which first stood all alone like a brutalist obstruction on the then still-undeveloped waterfront. A sombre oil portrait of the paper's fallen leader, Joseph E. (Holy Joe) Atkinson, which previously hung in the executive suite, was put up in the lobby. Duncan Macpherson, the political cartoonist, would sometimes kidnap it and pretend to hold it for ransom. The painter had symbolized Atkinson's charitable work by showing him poised over his chequebook, pen in hand. Misanthropes looking at the picture said that the cheque was probably made out to *Cash*. In any case, at the *Star* of those days one could still sense a kind of closet bookishness in certain unlighted parts of the newsroom, the residue of the old Mechanics' Institute type of Liberal humanism so thoroughly associated with Atkinson.

For example, one of the photographers, Reg Inell, a fixture of the second-hand book trade, was an English utopian socialist who had put together one of the world's outstanding private collections of Shelley (but never got around to publishing the bibliography that was supposed to result). Among the innumerable assistant managing editors was one named Ray Gardner, another socialist, who was also passionate about collecting. Perhaps the most learned (and least demonstrative) example was Borden Spears. He was a trained classicist. At the time, however, he was serving as managing editor, perhaps as a stopgap measure until the next piece of meat in Martin Goodman's carnivorous career could be brought in for sacrifice. I scarcely knew Spears, but he seemed to approve of me instinctively. So when Kildare sought a lengthy leave of absence, to have another whack at his African novel, I was asked to fill in for him on the book page until he returned.

Life had taken a definite upturn. I loved the *Star* and what it stood for (and still do, to the extent that it continues on the same course). And while I could never match Kildare's special gifts, I knew that it wasn't going to be difficult to make a favourable impression. Totally disdainful and suspicious of office politics as he was, Kildare had lost his assistant, and his space for reviews had been whittled down to a single page. I was able to keep alive the note of eccentricity while also acknowledging that we were working for the proprietors of Canada's biggest newspaper, not for Addison and Steele. Within the limits imposed by the seasonal nature of publishing, I tried to match the more generous and better-paying section at the *Globe* in reviewing the key books on their day of publication. A couple of times I even finagled an extra page in the weekend edition. I certainly brought in new writers and took pride in the fact that they were of all political stripes; for example, I got Barbara Amiel to do her first book review; it ran alongside ones by people as far to the left as she was to the right. I also conducted many interviews, as well as trying to cover publishing as a legitimate beat. I imposed a rule that at least 50 per cent of the titles reviewed had to be Canadian, and was attempting to come up with some formula for ensuring that female authors and reviewers were both represented fairly. The entertainment editor, a recent refugee from the *Telegram* and a nice man though devoid of noticeable ability, patted me on the back affectionately and more than once took me to lunch at a restaurant-ship moored in the harbour directly across the street (it later sank). One week I was actually given a surprise raise in salary, modest but effective. At length, Kildare returned, novelless again, and I stepped aside to spend a year freelancing almost full time for the entertainment department. I might be writing a book piece in the morning, going to a screening in the afternoon and reviewing one or even two musical events in the evening. I say almost full time because during this period I also went to work for *Books in Canada.*

By this time, Douglas Marshall had succeeded Val Clery as editor of the magazine. Douglas was slow-spoken and sad-looking, and he seemed to me to distrust the book world and its inhabitants, no doubt feeling they were highbrows and elitists. "You actually *believe* in all this stuff, don't you?" he said to me one day. By this stuff he meant Canadian literature. I had to confess. His own taste in such writing ran strongly in support of Donald Jack, an admitted humourist who wrote a seven-volume *roman-à-fleuve*. The individual novels in the sequence had titles such as *Three Cheers for Me*, *That's Me in the Middle* and *It's Me Again* and were incessantly being given the Stephen Leacock medal. After Douglas got Jack to review Timothy Findley's novel *The Wars*, Margaret Atwood responded that this was like getting Red Buttons to play Hamlet. Douglas enjoyed drinking beer at the Chez Moi and other little taverns near the *Books in Canada* office, so I was able to make some changes in the magazine.

One of *Books in Canada*'s continuing weaknesses is the lack of civility in its letters pages. Such vituperation and spitefulness, such name-calling! Marshall and all previous and most subsequent editors of the magazine have found this tone of voice a proof of sophistication, whereas I thought it was a form of provincialism, as there was no real discourse beneath the babble. For a while at least I was able to play it down, and to contextualize it a bit by calling the letters sections "Umbrage & Unction." While the letters had to be brought under control, the standard of reviewing, even if considered as journalism, had to be raised, it seemed obvious to me. But sometimes the tiniest attempts to enliven the copy were overruled by people with no ear for cleverness. When Marian Engel published her novel *Bear*, whose story involves a woman's sexual relationship with a big smelly bear in the woods, I sought to amuse readers destined otherwise to be bored by adding at the top an epigraph from Cole Porter: "Bears do it / Bees do it / Even educated fleas do it. . . ." During the 1970s and early 1980s, I would be only one of a long succession of writers who worked at *Books in Canada* under the original owners. A partial list would include the translator and anthologist Wayne Grady (he became editor for a while) and poets such as Fraser Sutherland and Pier Georgio Di Cicco (in the managing editor's spot). Di Cicco left *Books in Canada*, and the rest of the secular world, to join an order of Christian brothers. This was the subject of great merriment, but I admired his decision as I couldn't possibly see myself doing anything so useful. I could only shake my head at the callowness of those who mocked him.

These two affiliations, the *Star* and *Books in Canada*, while themselves only part of a complex matrix of assignments and deadlines and publishing projects, kept me quite busy on their own. Too busy in fact.

Often when I stopped in at the *Star* in the year following his leave of absence, Kildare would report to me that his tolerance of the place was eroding. He said to me once that he had seen one of the executive assistants struggling to move a huge and sadly wilted potted plant into the newsroom.

"That's the sorriest specimen of *Ficus elastica* I've ever seen in my life," he remarked.

"Yes," she had replied without irony. "It's been in

the publisher's office. I think I've got it out of there just in time."

So Kildare announced one day that he was quitting to pursue the life of a roving travel essayist, a position that I can now see his work was groping towards. I wasn't surprised when the entertainment editor offered me the staff position of book-page editor, for which I would have to relinquish *Books in Canada* and various other outside entanglements. No sooner had I accepted than I was surprised, however, very much so, by how much the atmosphere at the *Star* changed. Borden Spears had stepped aside and the newly arrived managing editor was an Australian from *Time* in New York who had worked in Canada years earlier. One of his first orders of business was getting rid of me. His opening tactic was to activate the booby trap of bureaucracy. Theoretically there were four levels of authority between the book page and the ME: the assistant entertainment editor, the entertainment editor, the Saturday editor, and a deputy managing editor. They all began pressing for favourite hockey books or else finding fault with what was written about instead. I was doing the same job I had done a year earlier, when I had been liked and praised, and doing it precisely the same way, with the same emphasis on Canadian writing, but now with the Tasmanian Devil, as he was sometimes called behind his back, I was clearly marked for disposal. In his malevolently innocent way, the entertainment editor told me as much—that he'd been ordered to build up a paper trail, that it was just my bad luck that Spears had gone. In the space of a few months, I had five or six columns killed outright—more than one would expect to see spiked in a very long and contentious career. Such was the atmosphere of intimidation and fear at the paper that I got little support from the other people in the department. Not even the office mooch, Frank Rasky, who could claim once having received a letter from H.L. Mencken but who had been going downhill professionally for a generation, could be seen to take up my cause. Ken McGoogan, the long-serving book editor of the Calgary *Herald*, reminded me recently that he was a *Star* intern at the time and that I gave him his start as a reviewer; he said I always seemed depressed by the office politics.

I refused to quit and waited to be fired, which I was. The explanation I was given was that I didn't write well enough (a charge I've heard all my life and am always willing to accept constructively). But later I was told by the entertainment editor who fired me—not long before the stress caught up with him and he died at his desk of a heart attack at fifty-two—what the managing editor's real reason was: the entertainment department already had one person who stuttered and emphatically didn't need another. Perhaps he felt that the two of us would start to bring in our stuttering relatives and co-religionists until the whole place was shut down by dysfluency. Anyway, the paper filled my place with Roy MacSkimming, who even then had had many different positions in publishing but had not much experience in journalism. We were told that he was paid exactly double what Kildare and I had received, presumably because he was Canadian-born.

I thought that the institution had shown incredible cruelty in trying to sandbag the life of a twenty-four- or twenty-five-year-old. But although the episode left me sad and cross for some time afterwards, I was not really embittered by it. I took no joy in the news that the Tasmanian Devil didn't last much longer than I did, but went to New York to edit Rupert Murdoch's New York *Post*, which thereupon entered a glory period that is encapsulated, in the memories of many, by the front-page effusion HEADLESS BODY IN TOPLESS BAR (a headline destined to become so notorious that it became the title of a rather poor Hollywood movie in the 1990s). I am no respecter of Alexander Hamilton, being an Aaron Burr man myself and the proud possessor of a copy of Gore Vidal's novel *Burr* inscribed "from one old Burrite to another." Yet I remember remarking at the time how the *Post* had been founded by Hamilton in 1801 but then, in the short span of less than a hundred and seventy-five years, had deteriorated to the point of being edited by the T.D. Though not for very long, as it happened. The next time I saw him, the T.D. was a consultant, looking for client papers whose brows he could lower. I let slip that my brother was an editorial executive at Times-Mirror in Los Angeles and watched his attitude turn from derision to collegiality. I think of the seventies as a time of such hypocrisy.

Devotion to candour compels me to recall that for the remainder of the decade, or so it seems to me now, I was always either the villain or the hero of the moment. The reasons had a lot to do with the nature of journalism, with its romantic and rather theoretical fondness for renegades but its genuine love of corporate conformers, and with my own make-up too. I wasn't constructed temperamentally to stand the constant ricocheting from approval to dismissal and back again, yet for the same reason I couldn't seem to avoid it. Almost everybody else I knew in the trade was a salaried soldier. Most were happily so. I seemed to be quite different: a mercenary with principles: most definitely not a *samurai* but a *ronin*. An untenable contradiction. As a result, I was never quite accepted by the profession that was nonetheless my only means of support, since I was cut off from the other ways that writers have of making a living. This curious situation led me to think seriously for several years about the nature, problems and function of journalism. Eventually I would begin writing media criticism, and in time I produced a couple of books that I hoped traced the root causes of the journalistic malaise. One of these, *The Rise of the Canadian Newspaper*, sold quite acceptably as an Oxford University Press paperback and may have had some slight influence.

———————

Arletty, the French actress of the 1920s, whose films were part of the silent cinema that I studied with such autodidactic rigour in London, used to say that her background was not working class exactly but *original*. So too my own. In a previous memoir, *Travels by Night*, I wrote of Big Bill Lias, the crime lord of northern West Virginia and western Pennsylvania (the region where I had been held captive by my childhood). I told how Big Bill was (and is) revered as a folk hero. I recalled how he was succeeded in his position, though never in the people's affections, by a gambler named Paul Hankish, who gave me my first real job, as a kind of hanger-on apprentice in his gang, even before I broke into journalism at sixteen.

For reasons that will suddenly seem less obscure in a moment, I pause again to remember this pair of hoodlums who were quite different from each other in their criminal gifts and their approach to the Life. Lias was tremendously smart and clever: vulpine of mind however bovine his girth. He provided patrons with facilities for craps, roulette, whatever they fancied, but his forte was running barboot, a game well known in the Greek neighbourhoods of South Wheeling whence the Big Guy originated. The virtue of barboot was that players tested their skill and luck against one another, not against the house. All bets had to be covered by another player, so that equal amounts of money were sliding across the table between winners and losers. This attracted serious gamblers from throughout the country who enjoyed seeing hundreds of thousands of dollars in play in a genuine test of ability, secure in the understanding that all the appropriate authorities had been paid to look the other way. Readers will find references to Wheeling's magnetic appeal in the gambling literature, such as Richard Jessup's 1963 novel *The Cincinnati Kid*.

In Wheeling barboot, the house would take only a minuscule piece of the flow, usually 1.5 per cent. The house was therefore a straight one, content in its systemic incorruptibility to make profits from a level reputation (and also from the quality of its drinks and entertainment).

Lias, I am certain, foresaw the nationalization of gambling in the form of state lotteries, and felt that his stress on excitement, good food and floor shows was the surest hedge against the ravages of too much government. Hankish, who came out of Wheeling's Lebanese community, which was one of the largest in the country, had different traditions and approaches. Gambling itself was but one part of his criminal organization, and it inclined towards sports betting, sometimes on events, such as fights, which he himself promoted and to which he would control broadcast rights. He too was clever but differently, fighting against the legitimate private sector by trying to keep ahead of where it would be going in a few years' time.

Perhaps a generational difference is the distinction I'm searching for here. In any case, both men had kindly sides to their natures, and Paul Hankish, it developed, singled me out for some kind of adoption. He had plans for me. I knew instinctively that he was grooming me to be what he was—which would have made me the last of the Wheeling gamblers, I suppose. He took time to talk with me and learn my interests and explain some of his doings. This meant that he thought I was smart, that I had brains. He was the first such person I had encountered, the first to sense that I was by no means so dumb as I sounded (a physiological impossibility perhaps), or even so dumb as I looked. Anyway, I fear that I let Paul down when I decided to become a writer instead, and years went by before I met another person who had the exact same faith in my abilities and could hear me somehow with my own inner voice rather than the halting one with which I communicated out loud. That individual was Robert Fulford, the lively and intelligent Toronto essayist and person-about-the-arts, who once, in a rare moment of ambiguous hyperbole, likened my arrival in Toronto to that of Hurricane Hazel a dozen years earlier.

When I first saw him, Bob was poised to become the editor of *Saturday Night*. He was six feet tall and fleshy, with a big oval face full of kindness and curiosity: a large man, like his father Ab, a Roman Catholic who had left the church to marry Bob's mother and who had worked for the Canadian Press in Toronto during the Depression and the war, in the days when everyone kept a bottle of rye in the drawer. In his office Bob had a photograph of Ab that he was slowly coming to resemble. Bob was only in his mid-thirties at the time I am thinking of now. But watching his hair recede was like watching some slow war of attrition against determined insurgents: the line of demarcation was forever being erased and then redrawn a little farther back on his head. By the time I came into his life, only a very few stray hairs still held out bravely below the 38th Parallel.

Years later, in his memoir *Best Seat in the House*, he would write that he was only ever "an intellectual among journalists and a journalist among intellectuals." In fact, he was that third thing, an intellectual who wrote to be read by a wider audience, a journalist in that sense but one whose beat, so to speak, was abstract ideas—the ideas that moved politics and social trends and culture in all its forms. He was a public critic, a public questioner, in a straight line of descent from, to take two wildly dissimilar examples, Edmund Wilson and Dwight Macdonald. But the tradition was much older than any of its few modern practitioners could suggest. Bob was a freelance intellectual, operating beyond and beneath the universities, non-aligned and unattached, and he never lost his fascination with being alive, with being part of the spectacle that he found himself in the middle of.

Born as he was in 1932, he had come along at precisely the right moment to chronicle Canada's cultural awakening and be a vital part of it at the same time. He was a self-made cosmopolite, though a bit too Torontocentric, as everyone elsewhere in Canada was forever contending, quite rightly. No matter, he had the knack of making today the right time and wherever he was the right place to be. For example, he had attended, as *Down Beat*'s Toronto representative, the single most famous jazz concert of the age, when Charlie Parker, Dizzy Gillespie, Charlie Mingus, Bud Powell and Max Roach jammed on the stage at Massey Hall in 1953. When the Beatles came to Maple Leaf Gardens a dozen years later, it was Fulford they asked to be interviewed by. He was also an important explainer of Canadian painting, and did much to make the reputations of certain visual artists of his generation—artists such as Harold Town, Joyce Wieland, Michael Snow, William Ronald. Some have worn better than others, of course. The point is only that Bob seemed to be part of whatever was new, even though he was squarely in the humanist tradition that took its nourishment from the accumulated past. He had been on *This Hour Has Seven Days* when it remade the way Canadians watched television. He was among the most gifted film critics of the kind I think of as being not like consumer advocates but rather like haruspices—those holy men in Ancient Rome who read the times by inspecting the entrails of chickens and other sacrificial creatures. That is, the relationship, both passive and active, between cinema and society is what interested him, though movies were always a secondary interest to literature and politics. He wrote most of his many film reviews and essays under the pseudonym Marshall Delaney, combining his own middle name with the surname of a great aunt, Theresa Delaney, co-author of *Two Months in the Camp of Big Bear* (1885), a minor primary document in the literature of the North-West Rebellion. How entirely appropriate for someone so concerned with distilling the context from the moment that, when Bob became the *second* published author in the family, his first book should have been an excited one about Expo 67.

There were other books later—mostly collections of columns and pieces, including one called *Marshall Delaney at the Movies*, which I browbeat him into assembling and found a publisher for. But despite my nagging, he never became a book writer primarily.

"Publishing books is why God put us here," I remember pleading with him finally.

"A peculiar theology," he replied, "but one distinctively your own."

This indifference was the curse of being even a

non-journalist forced to make a living inside the institution of journalism—and it was one I myself was
determined to avoid if I could. It is also the sad devoir
of middle-class journalists and editors with families to
support, like Bob, who was then with his first wife,
Jocelyn Dingman, who descended from an old news-
papering family and was the mother of two.

When Bob went to work as a copy boy at the
*Globe and Mail* in 1949, he knew a very old man who
had once been a copy boy for Edmund E. Sheppard,
the Americophilic troublemaker and professional
eccentric who had founded *Saturday Night* in 1887
(and later became editor of the *Star*). There was thus
a certain rightness about the rumours of Bob's
appointment to *Saturday Night*, but rightness on
more solid ground than this alone. The magazine had
had at least one famous editor, whose reign, from 1932
to 1951, was the magazine's heyday, its golden age.
Like Bob, B.K. Sandwell was an arts-lover and an
instinctive liberal, proud of what he stood four-square
against as well as of what he supported instinctively.
"I never met anyone who worked on the *Telegram*
who has the least bit of talent," I once heard Bob say,
ignoring all the conspicuous exceptions to this statement. "This," he said, with a chestful of old-time
*Toronto Daily Star* boasting, "is my equivalent of
racial prejudice." But Bob's own liberalism was a rela-
tive thing, as liberalism tends to be. He would always
oppose censorship (he had led the fight against the
arrest of the Toronto art dealer Dorothy Cameron in
the 1960s and was forever testifying in defence of free
speech), and though he came to embrace Canadian

nationalism intensely for a few years either side of 1970, he later disavowed it by his words and actions, as so many others were doing as the decade rolled to a close. Indeed, he became a supporter of Free Trade, though not actually a Mulroneyite. And I don't think he ever quite got to the point of putting property rights over human rights. During much of the 1970s he was also a loud and sincere proponent of feminism, including radical feminism, but found he had to keep his support a private feeling once feminists began telling him to shut up as he had no part or say in the subject, which they said was simply none of his business. As for his continentalism, I was terribly sorry to see him return to the pro-American stream in which he had swum as a boy, but I thought I understood his motive at least. He was always a fervent anti-communist, having reached his majority in the early 1950s after all. Yet he was also deeply wounded, he told me years later, by America's errand in Vietnam—because it so thoroughly destroyed his illusions about the U.S., the U.S. he grew up with (but where he'd never lived, only visited).

All of which is to say that I found that politics made conversation between us difficult, or at least brought it to a clumsy turn sometimes. I was always at odds with, and embarrassed by, Bob's view of pro-U.S. corporatism, as he was with, and by, my own. In one of the few signs of ill-temper I ever saw him exhibit, he once threw me out of his office for saying that Ho Chi Minh was obviously so much better educated than Lyndon Johnson—a statement not in the least asinine in the context of whatever we had been discussing, and also true, of course; most higher primates are better rounded than Lyndon was. Another time, years later, I accidentally drove him near apoplexy by letting drop the theory that anomalies in John F. Kennedy's assassination start to explain themselves away if you simply embrace the possibility that Lee Harvey Oswald was the Messiah: a low-life Galilean, his pockets full of self-destructive expectations, who wandered from the distant margins of society into the centre of events much bigger than himself: a young fellow who got mixed up with the Romans and paid the price by getting nailed. (Thinking back now, I will qualify my remarks to the point of saying that at the very least the lives of Oswald and Jesus have one lesson in common: whatever you do, keep away from the Romans.)

In other words, I discovered Bob's politics growing less and less like my own as we got older, but I was careful never to let this influence our friendship. One can't pick one's friends on the basis of their political affiliations. Certainly I can't (in my capacity as an Oswaldian liberal), or I'd be a very lonely fellow indeed. What I'm getting at here is that Bob was often compared and contrasted to Sandwell, that exemplar of Montreal *Star* liberalism. But Bob's own favourite among the old editors of *Saturday Night* was Sandwell's predecessor, Hector Charlesworth, who held the post from 1926 to 1932. Today, alas, Charlesworth is remembered almost entirely for being the cultural reactionary who couldn't make sense of the Group of Seven and didn't hesitate to say so again and again—for that and for his eerie physical resemblance

to Edward VII. But the cognoscenti know Charlesworth was no philistine. The people who hunt for sus-
tenance in the netherworld of the second-hand
bookstores cherish his three volumes of memoirs,
*Candid Chronicles, More Candid Chronicles* and *I'm
Telling You*: taken together, a priceless source of anec-
dote—much of it wrong, unfortunately—from the
political, journalistic, theatrical, musical and criminal
worlds of Canada from the late 1870s to the start of
the Great Depression.

Bob took over *Saturday Night* in the late 1960s,
and by the 1970s, when I became a regular (to some,
indeed, an annoying) fixture of its pages, he had put
his own stamp on it and was beginning to gallop. He
had very little money to pay writers. So he improved
the magazine by spotting young talent whose eager-
ness for a place to write as they wished far outweighed
any sumptuary considerations. Everyone appeared at
least once, it seemed to me, though not always in the
clothing for which they would become better known
later. Many years before he was Marshall McLuhan's
biographer, the *Star* books columnist or a writer of
thrillers, Philip Marchand was recognized primarily
for his articles on pop sociology in Fulford's *Saturday
Night*. Before I extended my troublemaking into
other areas of prose, I was known to a small but fierce
readership for my reviews and round-ups of Canadian
poetry at the back of the magazine. The artist Michael
Snow, of all people, took me to task for once using up
the entire book section with a piece on Louis Dudek's
relationship to Ezra Pound. Snow was offended, feeling that reviewing one book in depth and at length,

instead of several superficially, was a misprision of journalistic common sense.

Slowly and by degrees a small cadre of talented people grew up around Bob's editorship. In hindsight, I think perhaps the most solid one as a journalist—the most thorough metabolizer of her research, the most deeply feeling and most meticulous inquirer—was Erna Paris, whose prose and personality were both nicely disciplined in the bargain. Another was Myrna Kostash, whom I've always found it impossible not to like, despite her public struggles down through the years with entertaining the notion that I might somehow be her equal as a human being. A third writer, a Winnipeger, was Heather Robertson, in whom one could see long generations of angry and austere Highland puritanism losing its piety, but none of its evangelical zeal, in the transformation to a fiery and secular political roundhead-ism. In 1975, she had scandalized some of the people who read *Maclean's* in barbershops and beauty parlours by confessing to "a desire to toss a hand grenade into every American camper I pass on the highway." Later, of course, her views matured 180 degrees. The transformation reminds me of a certain poet and visual artist who told me in the 1970s that I was too cozy with the Establishment for him to waste time on but who by the 1980s was accepting public-art commissions for the new Metro Police headquarters. In any case, Heather and I once had a pleasant conversation about how our politics had crossed in the night, headed in opposite directions.

And then there was Valerie Miner Johnson, or plain Valerie Miner as she's now known in the U.S. for her growing shelf of novels as well as for her non-fiction works on feminism. As I remember her, she belonged to that particular gene pool that causes sentimental people to say with wistful admiration, "Ah, she has the map of Ireland written on her face." She had already worked as a writer in the U.S. and in Britain and had come to Canada during the Vietnam excitement with her draft-aged husband: a circumstance and an atmosphere she captures perfectly in her 1982 novel, *Movement*. It was a great loss to Canada when she finally returned, husbandless, to the U.S., where she taught at Berkeley, Arizona State and elsewhere as she built her literary career, becoming eventually, I would think, one of the most important figures in contemporary American lesbian writing.

The four of them—Paris, Kostash, Robertson and Miner, together with a fifth writer, Melinda McCracken—worked collectively on a book of personality profiles entitled *Her Own Woman* (1975). Most if not all of these writers were among the founders of the Periodical Writers' Association of Canada. The 1970s was a time when Canadian writers were furiously organizing for self-protection, with bodies such as the Playwrights' Co-op and the League of Canadian Poets and, most successfully and influentially of all, the Writers' Union of Canada. In the Union's formative stages, some of its activists, such as Marian Engel, wanted to limit membership to fiction writers—actually, to fiction writers whom they liked or agreed with. Fortunately, the non-exclusionary faction carried the day, and the Union became more and more powerful (and the need for a writers' group deeply rooted in social allegiance would lie dormant until the 1980s, when the Canadian branch of PEN was reactivated to serve this and other needs). But it was in this political environment of the 1970s that the people who made their livings writing their hearts out for magazines like *Saturday Night*, *Maclean's*, *Weekend*, *The Canadian*, *Quest* and the better newspapers, in what seemed an atmosphere of constant slipperiness, disappointment, even deceit at times, themselves decided to band together. At first, the organization was to be for women only, but after the initial meeting Valerie and a couple of others asked me to lunch in order to compare notes about fees and other information, to gather evidence in case it should turn out that the editors were systematically discriminating against female contributors. When the subject of *Saturday Night* came up, Valerie said that Bob was paying her as much as $700 for a piece.

"You deserve it," I said, "but I have to tell you that after all these years he's never paid me more than three."

People decided from the beginning, then, that the new organization should be open to all professional magazine freelancers, regardless of gender. The organization retained some currency, and even a little clout, so long as the magazine industry itself stayed vibrant and competitive in the face of imported Americanism, which wasn't for so long as all of us wished with such fervour. Although PWAC still exists, it is more analogous to the Canadian Authors' Association. I don't say this unkindly. I mean only that it tends to embrace many part-time or hobbyist writers and that certainly it is no longer a militant organization pressing for changes in the rules (except in the all-important matter of copyright).

In those days, magazines tended to be centred in the lower part of downtown, where Toronto's first Lichtman's newsstand also happened to be. It was the only place in the city to stock a full array of foreign newspapers and arcane, obscure, out-of-the-way or otherwise hard-to-find magazines. The shop was a hole-in-the-wall on the north side of Adelaide, a few steps west of Yonge, and every day it would be crowded with writers and editors, coming and going.

One afternoon in 1975 or 1976 I stopped there on my way to or from a meeting with Bob at *Saturday Night*. The store was especially crowded, and as I left I almost literally ran into a man on crutches who was trying to enter. I saw his face for only a second, but I made him instantly. It was Paul Hankish from Wheeling. (Later, I deduced that, as this incident took place during the racing season at Fort Erie, he was doubtless visiting Canada for recreational purposes and was perhaps in search of a copy of the *Daily Racing Form*.) I resisted—but just barely—the natural urge to call out his name and re-introduce myself. I still had my instincts if not my wits about me. I knew that to say out loud, "Paul, Paul Hankish, my God, it's really you, how are you doing?" in a public place was, in his circle, a *faux pas* of almost inexpressible seriousness. "So, how did you make out on that grand jury thing I read about?" I could hear myself babbling on, dangerously. Instead, the non-meeting was over in an instant. As I pushed outside, he pushed in, not recognizing the former kid from so long ago. I waited a few minutes up the street until he emerged with a paper under his arm and climbed, with difficulty, into the back of the long black car waiting at the curb. The windows were tinted so you couldn't see in. He vanished in the one-way traffic like an artefact being buried in the blowing sand.

———————

Looking back with the lucidity that is supposed to come with the passage of so much time, I still find it difficult to know just what went wrong between Rachel and me. To be sure, we found ourselves separated by rhetorical differences. She had been reared in a theatre of guilt in which I refused to play an assigned role. Rather than deny blame, I would always accept it with eager insincerity, as a selfish means of civilizing the discourse. This tactic is a weakness I have displayed all my adult life, during which I have cheerfully taken responsibility for the Fenian invasion, the failure of the Second Paris Commune, and the great Tokyo earthquake of 1923—anything to make my opponent shut the bloody hell up and return to the kind of dialogue that, to continue the stage metaphor, more closely resembles a highly personalized version of Noh theatre. That is to say, I've relied on the absurdly utopian notion that relationships can turn on subtlety, not bluntness. I was always working towards a domestic situation in which everything is so static (read peaceful) that any change whatever (a raised eyebrow, a cleared throat) would take on exaggerated—but, to me, unmistakably clear—meaning. Its very nature made this a vision that was easier to strive for oneself, or to suggest by example, than it was to explain, much less to propagate. For her birthday, I had bought Rachel a puppy from the Humane Society on Wellesley Street, a terrier mix I called Heywood, because her big ears and dishevelled appearance gave her a resemblance to Heywood Broun of the New York *World*, the co-founder of the Newspaper Guild. Rachel quickly lost interest and was always talking about how the dog could be given away "to a farmer." Similarly, Rachel considered me a failure as a human being and our household unworkable. I suspected that she was desperately trying to find a farmer on whom to unload me as well. "He'll be happier in the country," I could hear her thinking. "He'll have a place to run."

One Saturday afternoon she returned from a walk to say that she had just been to bed with Jim Christy, expecting me to react with possessive outrage. But sexual jealousy isn't among my many conspicuous faults, and this too angered her (and also, for some reason, Christy, who for the next decade or so would attack me in print whenever the opportunity arose, though Rachel and he never became a couple and as far as I could determine he had no stake in the matter one way or another). Shortly thereafter Rachel experienced what she later described as a vision. For hours she lay on the bed in the most agitated emotional state, weeping with excitement while keeping perfectly still, as though possessed by some benevolent demon or transfixed by a penetrating look into the future. "This is your last chance to be loved," she told me. This was a shocking possibility, but for the life of me I couldn't figure out what I was supposed to do, how exactly I was expected to change when what was being asked for was not some cosmetic adjustment but an actual chemical alteration.

Rachel went west, sending back notes that grew progressively shorter and shorter tempered, until finally silence seemed my only option. I kept Heywood, who had a good innings, living until 1987, *aet* fifteen, when she died in my arms. Rachel threw over literature, perhaps as a way of further washing her hands of me, and began a fresh existence in the film business. I've always prided myself on maintaining harmonious relations with former lovers, but in this case my overtures, at long intervals, have led nowhere, and I'm no closer to understanding the relationship now than I was when it ended. At the time, I could respond only by deciding to live alone and hurl myself into work. For more than a decade I was maybe the most obnoxiously ubiquitous independent writer in the city, at least insofar as the magazine and newspaper press were concerned. I experienced all the joy of the freelance life in that I was not able to avoid institutions exactly but at least was able to deal with them on my own terms, seldom having to tie myself down. But I suffered the freelancer's constant anxiety as well. Every experience, sight, person or idea had to be turned to account somehow. For a dozen years I never knew the luxury of an unexpressed thought.

*Saturday Night*'s history could only be called bizarre. Before he founded it as a Society weekly with antisocial tendencies, E.E. Sheppard, though Canadian, had gone to Bethany College in Virginia, the cradle of Campbellitism (the sect now called the Disciples of Christ). In the days before the Civil War, Bethany had been the favourite school for the errant sons of the Southern slave-holding aristocracy. Later Sheppard moved west and is said to have worked for a time as a stage coach driver on the frontier. Back in Toronto in the 1880s, he cultivated a southwestern appearance, with free-falling mustachios and the sort of long linen duster favoured by drovers and outlaws. He used the Spanish honorific *Don* as his pseudonym. He took great sport in, and drew deep reader response from, reviewing the sermons preached from every pulpit in the city. He reviewed them not as theology but as theatre, which is doubtless what they were.

The great days of *Saturday Night* were in the 1920s, 1930s and 1940s, when it was still a weekly—a folio-sized glossy-paper weekly that carried more advertising linage than any other North American publication of the same frequency (and there were many that tried to imitate its success). It was a wildly cosmopolitan affair then (the old files reveal contributions by writers as different as Bertrand Russell and Ben Hecht), but it did not circulate outside Canada because it seemed to touch something intrinsic to that elusive ectoplasm, the Canadian spirit. It represented an ideal—the general-interest and purely Canadian magazine—that had flourished for a while in *The Week* and, later, in the original *Canadian Magazine*.

Much later than these came the two glorious periods in the life of *Maclean's*, immediately after the Second World War when it was edited by Arthur Irwin, the visionary of its greatness, and subsequently, when it was edited by Ralph Allen, the engine of its achievement.

In any case, *Saturday Night*, at its zenith, thought that it stood solidly for progress and for national fulfilment within the proper imperial context. It was also especially well regarded for its incorruptibly honest coverage of Bay and St James streets, which in those days were densely populated with bucket-shop operators, purveyors of phoney gold mines and all sorts of other characters. (After all, Carlo Ponzi, for whom the Ponzi scheme is named, first perfected this particular bunko in Canada before taking it to the States.)

After its fat days—roughly, the Sandwell years and a little before—*Saturday Night* would pass through many pockets of business turbulence. At one point it seemed to be owned by a group indistinguishable from the national executive of the Social Credit Party. Then it was bought by Jack Kent Cooke, who in partnership with the first Lord Thomson had made a fortune in broadcasting. Before departing permanently for the United States, where he became an impossibly wealthy sports impresario and was made a U.S. citizen retroactively by special act of Congress, Cooke had put a lot of money and effort into Consolidated Press, as the company that owned *Saturday Night* was called. With such other magazines as *Liberty* and *Canadian Homes and Gardens*, his firm was determined to give

Maclean Hunter, with its *Maclean's* and *Chatelaine*, a run for its money. The two establishments also had parallel stables of industrial and trade magazines, great money-spinners in those days.

Consolidated Press operated out of a building on Richmond near Bay that had once been the printing plant of the *Star*. Hugh Garner, who worked for both *Saturday Night* and *Liberty* during the reign of Cooke, who became his protector, recreates the atmosphere in his fiction a couple of times. Going there today you can still see an elaborate wrought-iron cartouche with *Saturday Night's* logo in the railing of the staircase in the lobby. In time, I suppose, Cooke must have found himself in the same position as Wyatt Earp who, in forsaking Dodge City for Tombstone, is reported to have said, "This town is losin' its *snap*." When, accordingly, Cooke blew the pop-stand that is Toronto, Consolidated was broken into its component pieces. *Saturday Night* was purchased by its editor, Arnold Edinborough, the somewhat tweedy and (many believed) somewhat pompous arts supporter and influential Anglican layperson whose career, including the editorships of both *Saturday Night* and, before that, the Kingston *Whig-Standard*, owed everything to his friendship with Robertson Davies and the Davies family.

When Fulford published *Best Seat in the House* in 1988, he surprised many people by his acid comments on a number of his colleagues and contemporaries. The tone of such remarks seemed completely out of character with his known personality. For example, he took swipes at Beland Honderich, the publisher of the *Star*, who by giving him a daily column in the country's biggest newspaper had made him a presence in the cultural life of the country in a way that neither his position at *Maclean's* nor any of his other jobs could have done. Bob was also pretty hard on Edinborough, who in *his* memoirs, a few years later, did not descend to the same level. Instead, Edinborough would recall how, having bought *Saturday Night* from Cooke, he decided that being both publisher and editor was too big a task, that as much as it hurt him to give up the half he preferred, he had no doubt but that Fulford was the better qualified person to be editor. This is the point in its life when I began to observe the magazine at close range.

In my time *Saturday Night* has occupied, I believe, nine different sets of offices, some seedy and humble, some trendy and grand. My first visits were to a very tiny suite of rooms in the Prudential Building at 55 York Street, round the corner from the Royal York Hotel, an old-fashioned skyscraper with a few touches of *moderne* and watered-down deco. No. 55 was then occupied largely by lone-wolf lawyers, distributors of down-market clothes for kiddies, import-export firms and commission sales agents. *Saturday Night* had a square reception area with tiny offices along three sides. The first thing that greeted visitors was a tall bookcase that seemed to tell the sad story of the magazine's long decline. Up in the top left corner were a number of monthly volumes of the early *Saturday Night*, bound in black morocco. The magazine was then folio-sized. Soon it had slipped to tabloid, while adhering to its original frequency. The volumes representing this period featured only simple cloth "library" bindings. Then the frequency had changed and *Saturday Night*, about the fourth shelf from the top, was a thin weekly in the same format as much thicker competitors such as *Maclean's* or the *Saturday Evening Post*. Latterly, it had gone down to what was called *Time*-size, and was thin and weak from loss of blood. Piles of the recent issues, no longer worth binding up each year, were tossed pell-mell along the bottom shelf. The spectacle was not inspiring. The story of *Saturday Night* in contemporary times was like a Buddhist version of Hell in which the magazine kept being reincarnated as some lower and lower form of life.

One of the cheap doors hid the office of Edinborough, who would sometimes stand in the middle of the reception room and call together the rest of the staff to hear him read his publisher's column for that month. I've maintained a much higher level of respect for Edinborough and his good works than Bob did, but it was clear that what had always held Edinborough back, in his various cultural endeavours, was simply that he never learned how to write well enough to cause anyone to wish to read him. Bob, who had an office about the size of four coffins, grimaced at Edinborough's tactics, which included hiring a public-relations firm to set up radio interviews and press coverage whenever he travelled out of town to give some talk on the latest debate about revisions to the prayer book or some other vital issue of the moment. Bob's own cubby-hole overlooked York Street, a boulevard in repose. As if to prove the point, there were two extremely poor eating-places there that we sometimes patronized: a mock-Bavarian joint called the Oom-pah-pah Room and, down at the end of the street, the Walker House, located in an octagonal brick structure from the mid-nineteenth century, built originally as a cyclorama, in which patrons could stand in the centre of realistic 360-degree paintings of—I don't know specifically—but let us say the Silver Jubilee of Queen Victoria or some triumph over the Boers in the South African War. Bob was sometimes mildly depressed at these meetings, the way I suppose I had seemed to Ken McGoogan at the *Star* when brought up against the inherent limitations in my situation. But Bob's outlook improved considerably when Edinborough sold out to William Nobleman, an advertising salesman and aspiring politician, with, I think, some injections of capital from Arthur Gelber, part of the Gelber family of local arts patrons. Nobleman was a decent chap but also an incredible scissor-bill, or so it seemed to me back then, in my judgemental middle twenties. He once asked me to read over the speech he proposed to deliver to the nomination meeting in the riding he was hoping to represent for the Conservatives. I made a few suggestions. He pressed me for my own party affiliation. I said that I never exercised the franchise, as I felt that voting for politicians tended to give them encouragement. Poor Mr Nobleman was shocked, shocked. He had never before encountered such disregard for the fundamentals of civic responsibility. I probably didn't support the militia either. We didn't go into the matter.

*Saturday Night* in the early Fulford period was nothing like the periodical it would become during the second half of his long reign there. In the old days it was a magazine of the arts and public affairs, often in that order. It was very slender and obviously produced on a shoestring. The audience climbed slowly from about seventy thousand when Bob arrived to a hundred thousand in a few years' time: great progress but of course not nearly great enough. *Saturday Night* was a mass medium, but just barely. Media buyers and account execs at the ad agencies never liked or understood it. Although this made its continued existence a constant worry, it also gave Bob a wonderful freedom to do as he pleased, which is no doubt what lured him there in the first place—that and a desire to be more of a national figure than the *Toronto Daily Star*, for all its monolithic dominance of the local market, could make him. Always careful not to keep all of his eggs in a single basket so fragile as *Saturday Night*, whose fate hinged perpetually on one wealthy backer or another, Bob began a weekly arts column for the *Star*; it also appeared in the Ottawa *Citizen* and sometimes other papers as well. And he still kept, and worked hard at, his late-night weekly CBC Radio programme, *This Is Robert Fulford*. (The founding producer was Geraldine Sherman. They later married, following his divorce from Jocelyn Dingman, and had two children before Geraldine quit the CBC to write fiction and perform good works.)

When people mistook his curiosity and vital energy for a desire to monopolize opinion, Bob would respond with dry humour.

"I pause to assess my situation," he said to me one day. "I edit the only extant magazine that quite literally hasn't made a penny's profit since 1949. I write a syndicated column that isn't really syndicated. I am also the host of a radio show that comes on so late on Saturdays that most everyone in Canada, even the Baptists, are already making love. I ask you: In a democratic society, like that to which all honest persons aspire, is it right for one man to have all this power?"

His wit was one of the great pleasures of his company. Like most journalists, he had an ear for what I like to call crop reports (gossip is who's sleeping with whom, which doesn't interest me, whereas crop reports—news of who's now in what job and why—are as vital to culture as they are to agriculture). When Bob gave you the day's commodity prices, he would do the voices of all the principal characters and sometimes rise from his chair to imitate their movements with gusto and satiric precision. He was quick with an ad-lib, too. One day he asked what had become of a certain prominent Liberal whose name seemed to have dropped off the roster without anyone noticing. I opined that the figure in question was occupying that Mackenzie King Chair of Government that the Rockefellers had funded at Harvard. "My God," he exploded. "The Mackenzie King Chair of Government! That's like someone endowing a Jack the Ripper Chair of Women's Studies!" He was always bipartisan in his amusement with politics. If he lacked fond adolescent memories of Prime Minister King, he saved his most biting words of weariness for John Diefenbaker, whose bluster and buffoonery, he said quite seriously, used to make him ashamed to admit his own nationality to strangers while travelling abroad.

Bob was the last person you would think of as a deliberate eccentric in the manner of *Saturday Night*'s beloved founder. Rather, he was, in the best sense, a straight arrow. "The essence of middle-class morality," he used to say, quoting Auden, "is payment of bills by return of post." Once he parted with Edinborough, this attitude must have been the only painful part of being the editor of the magazine; I remember his angst—though that's scarcely an adequate word—when *Saturday Night* bounced a contributor's cheque to Morley Callaghan. But I would go further than this in describing Bob's reliability. Starting in the early 1980s, psychologists who studied the offspring of alcoholics began pointing out that such children are likely to share a number of characteristics in later life. They may judge themselves constantly with an unnatural and unhealthy strictness (as I think Bob tended to do). Also, they're likely to be either totally irresponsible or hyper-responsible in their day-to-day dealing with the world. Bob certainly was the latter. I'd go so far to say that he was obviously the kind of person one would wish to take over the parenting of one's kids if one were killed in an air crash. Yet while my affection for him is deep and genuine, I cannot gainsay that he possessed traits that could be viewed as eccentric if wrenched out of the context by someone who didn't know him.

For example, Bob was totally, sometimes hilariously, ungifted in particular areas of locomotion and outdoor activity. Long after everyone else had moved to electric typewriters, he still produced his prodigious output on an old Underwood No. 5 that looked as if it was made of cast iron. His fingers would blur as they moved across the keyboard at superhuman speed. In fact, though, he didn't type any more accurately than I did at my much slower pace, and all his letters had to be retyped by a professional, though he compensated for this by being the most careful proofreader I've ever known. But then he was left-handed. In my experience and observation, the most attentive proofreaders, like the most successful assassins, are always left-handed: they've been born with a self-assigned mission to bring order to a world hell-bent on entropy.

I think of other examples of this disregard for economic common sense, such as the fact that he never learned to drive an automobile. Geraldine had once tried to teach him, and she took him out for some practice on a country road. Far off in the distance Bob saw another car approaching, menacingly he believed, and so he drove into a ditch. Accordingly, he took taxis everywhere, and sometimes, if we were headed off in the same direction, he would invite me to share. In this way I became aware that, in his morning taxi trip to the office, he would sometimes drop off a bag of his shoes at the shoeshine stand in the basement of the Park Plaza Hotel and pick up the work at five o'clock, on his way back north, running inside while the driver, double-parked on Bloor Street, made the evening traffic tie-up even worse than usual. As someone who was always trying to improve his level of self-reliance, I was pleasantly mystified by this ritual.

On Monday mornings, Bob would taxi to a certain newsstand where he could be among the first in Toronto to get copies of *The Sunday Times* and *The Sunday Telegraph*, which had come in from London by commercial aircraft. He did this in order to see what the line-up was in the various book review sections. All the old-time Toronto cabbies knew Bob by name and habits. But these runs astonished even one veteran—in my memory, it was a Diamond driver named Moe Lipton, who I dare say had seen all the extremes of human behaviour in his back seat over the years. "You mean you run up a twenty-dollar fare like this just to see what books have come out in England?" asked Moe, chewing on one of his foreshortened cigars. Moe was naturally incredulous.

This quite genuine faux-eccentricity, which was very complex, found its most complete expression, I believe, at *Saturday Night* itself—not in the published magazine necessarily (though I do remember with a shudder one entire issue devoted to a jeremiad by the satiric broadcaster and professional gadfly Larry Zolf). I mean, rather, in the staff. Bob inspired Gurkha-like loyalty in those who worked for him, freelancers as well as salaried employees, and many stayed a long time. One of these was his secretary or assistant, who was later hired by Peter C. Newman to be *his* secretary at *Maclean's*, only to be dumped in a few weeks' time. Bob felt the woman had been misused, and this may be one of the sources of his sour attitude towards Newman (also evident in *Best Seat in the House*), a one-sided feud that I have tried to patch

up over the years but without success. Despite people's sense of commitment to the publication, though,
the turn-over at *Saturday Night* was generally fairly
high, as one might expect in a magazine whose financial health was always precarious, and so Bob had fre-
quent opportunities to hire. While I have the greatest
respect for the cream of this cumulative editorial pla-
toon (you know who you are), I can't forget some of
Bob's near-misses.

For years, he had one editor who thought I was
mentally handicapped, or at least hearing-impaired,
because of my stutter. She never addressed me except
in a very loud voice, using words of only one or two
syllables, and employing such extreme gestures and
body language as she thought were needed to get her
meaning across. After the one re-employed by Peter
Newman came a long series of Bob's personal assistants, some superb, others not, including a person in
her twenties of whom I think Bob was frightened. She
never reacted to any outside stimulus—say, a ringing
telephone, a sudden movement or simply someone
speaking to her—without a kind of breathless anxiety
that bordered on a genuine panic and that, through
time, came to be seen as a kind of psychodrama. I
remember being in Bob's office at about four-thirty
one Friday when he asked me to look outside and see
if this person's coat and handbag were anywhere in
evidence. I peeked out and reported that they were
not in sight and that what's more the chair was empty
and the desk-top clean. This meant it was safe for him
to go home without any risk of conversation with her.
I seem to recall that this was the summer that Bob

wore a rather large Panama hat. As he was walking through the office one day, someone remarked admiringly that it made him look like Mark Twain. Bob frowned. Someone else said no, it made him look like Henry James. Bob beamed broadly. Another trend in his hiring practices is that through the late 1970s and into the 1980s, as he himself became more interested in conservatism, he tended to give jobs to people who were even more conservative than himself, perhaps to act as buffers or boundary-markers, I'm not sure. And then there were many people whom he simply inherited. *Saturday Night*'s bookkeeper, that is, the person in charge of stalling creditors and kiting cheques, was a fellow who, in a subsequent job in another industry, would be brought up on a fraud charge, only to be let off with probation after pleading that cocaine addiction had muddied his sense of right and wrong. He was the son of a woman who had worked for years in *Saturday Night*'s circulation department and who kept getting various other members of her family involved in the business—doing custodial or catering jobs, for example. Bob said he expected to come in one morning and find one of the innumerable collateral relatives had taken over as editor. And for years, the art director was Craig Allen, who had been a member of the legendary Toronto rock band of the 1960s called the City Muffin Boys—legendary in the sense of being elusive, because the musicians seemed never to turn up for their dates and were well known without actually being heard. For the eighty-fifth anniversary issue in December 1972, Craig commissioned a drawing of Her Majesty the Queen flushing herself down the loo, to illustrate an article by Leslie Hannon, an old *Maclean*'s hand, about the decline of monarchical feeling. I happened to be in Bob's office, listening to the latest crop reports, when he was thumbing through the vandykes and suddenly came to that page in the blue line. I'd never seen a heavy fellow move so fast as when Bob left off in mid-sentence and literally ran down the corridor to see if it were still possible to order a remake. It wasn't.

From time to time *Saturday Night* would throw parties in the office. On these occasions one would always see an elderly, out-of-place-looking man who, on being engaged in conversation, turned out to have had a far more interesting life than his appearance suggested. In the 1920s, for example, he had served on a British gunboat in China, chasing bandits and pirates. His connection to *Saturday Night* was that he wrote the monthly puzzle at the back of the magazine—had done so for decades. He was, in fact, the last known link to the great days of Sandwell: the age that Bob was starting to eclipse. Not financially. Far from it. But editorially and maybe in influence as well, though this may well be a mixed-fruit comparison, given that the two epochs are so different. The "old *Saturday Night*," as mature people still referred to Sandwell's magazine in those days, had been a powerful advertising vehicle and was an important voice in public affairs because it seemed to reach everyone across the country as only *Maclean*'s and the *Star Weekly* could also claim to do. Fulford's *Saturday Night* was always shaky economically, and it connected with a comparatively small audience. But it was a much deeper and more serious

read than the old magazine and, in its way, more stylish, too, though seldom slick and glib. Certainly
because of the increasing dominance of American
magazines, it came to be regarded as a much more
important institution culturally than it must have
seemed when it was primarily a successful business
rather than a precarious social service. Everyone who
was print-addicted appeared to have strong feelings
about it one way or the other. This phenomenon was
not accidental, but rather the result of what was going
on in Bob's mind sitting in the back of a traffic-stalled
taxi under the straw hat (or, in winter, a Russian-
looking fur one).

Bob surprised me once by saying that the essential
and elemental difference between magazine journalism and newspaper journalism is that the former, not
the latter, must be a creation of the moment it depicts
if it is to have any value at the time, much less later on.
He pointed to the fact that if you go back through the
microfilm of daily newspapers, you see that their
visual presentation has altered radically only a few
times over the centuries and that those changes were
mostly the result of new production technology. "But
look at a consumer magazine from ten years ago, or
five years ago, and its make-up and design will seem
just incredibly corny and old-fashioned. That's the test
of how successful it was in capturing the moment—
the fact that it stopped being fresh once the moment
had passed."

*Saturday Night* can be used to test the theory.
Returning to some of these issues I haven't had occasion to view in years, I find the very look of them

almost terrifyingly seventies. Through hard work (made harder by the size of the budget), Bob preserved some sense of the *magazine* as a *magasin*, a general store where readers shopped. He avoided the temptation to brainstorm cute visual ideas. The one exception to this avoidance of eye-catching tricks was a double-truck illustration that accompanied a piece about life on one of the cheap supermarket tabloids that were published in Quebec, mostly for the U.S. market. To show how interchangeable the stories in such publications were, Bob came up with six columns, running left to right: one of adjectives; a second of proper names, especially those of celebrities; a third and fourth of zesty verbs; and at the right, lists of appropriately inappropriate adjectives and the incongruous objects they modified. By mixing and matching, one could thus create tabloid headlines such as "Perverted Avon Lady Trips and Swears at Deformed Go-Go Dancer" or "Sex-Crazed Hippie Kills and Mutilates Well-to-Do Dental Technician." Generally, *Saturday Night* had no sidebars or annoying little bitty things to satisfy an audience more interested in television. It was that increasingly rare thing, a periodical for people who enjoyed reading. It was a matter of stubborn policy with Bob that stories, regardless of their length, run page-on until they were done, not jump from the island in the centre of the magazine to finish up in some stray column at the back-of-the-book, "among the truss ads."

Bob read all the mail each morning, even the press releases, before attacking the day's other publications, ranging, I remember, from *Foreign Affairs* to *Variety*.

Then it was on to the real work of editing. It was always a pleasure to have one of those meetings with him in which he dragged the visitor's chair round to his side of the desk, and you and he sat side by side going over a story a line at a time, looking critically at each sentence both in itself and in relation to what it contributed to the clockwork of paragraphs and pages. Even after all these years, I've seldom if ever met a more gifted line-editor. Another part of his day was spent on his large and incredibly diverse correspondence, including the fan letters he was famous for sending out to the young or obscure writers who had published, anywhere, something that caught his eye favourably. He also carried on extended exchanges with public and private figures about affairs of the day, including one series of letters, which went on for years, with someone he knew only through the mails—they avoided ever actually meeting lest they ruin their epistolary magic. Bob's correspondence will be seen as a treasure trove one day.

*Saturday Night* used ten-point Century as its body type, set in two wide columns, and the decks and treatments on the individual articles seemed to employ a great deal of a typeface named Cooper, or one of its close relatives. There was still a light visual aftertaste of the sixties in the way the extra-long serif of the *N* in *Night* (like one of the sideburns males wore at the time) descended below the logotype's eyeline, with just the faintest but trendiest suggestion of something psychedelic. In much the same way, the magazine then depended for illustration more on line drawings, such as those of Mike Constable and Martin

Vaughn-James, two figures from the Toronto under-ground press scene, than on commissioned photogra-phy. Other currents are just as expressive of the era and its transitions. By the point at which it began running my stuff (the most representative of which I later pre-served in a collection called *The Blue Notebook: Reports on Canadian Culture*), the magazine had given up on the idea of a London Letter but was still running an American Letter; this was written not by someone connected to the *Wall Street Journal* perhaps, as would seem natural later on, but by the socialist and peace activist David MacReynolds (whom I can remember hearing preach in New York years earlier—he had a pulpit style that I believe would have piqued the inter-est of Edmund E. Sheppard). Bob had enormous edi-torial common sense without being touched by the sort of low-browism that is almost always the negating flip side of such wisdom. Similarly, and what's at least as rare, he was in fact an intellectual who wasn't in the least pretentious. Through careful and invisible crafts-manship he made *Saturday Night* look a little bit ama-teurish, in an inviting, low-budget kind of way: neither an epic nor an art film but a Roger Corman movie perhaps, except unabashedly, gloriously and self-infatuatingly Canadian. What a wonderful place to write for. From it and a couple of other publica-tions, combined with a certain amount of undisguised (but blessedly unsigned) hack work, I was able to sub-sidize poetry and other bad habits, as a number of strange little publications from this period still attest.

Scanning my bookshelf now, I see, for instance, an obscure if not downright covert 1973 publication entitled *Café Terminus*. It was mimeographed in an edition of two hundred copies by Ed Jewinski, a poet who in those days was far less well known than his brother Hans, a police constable out of No. 52 Division. Hans had caught the public's fancy with *Poet Cop*, a mass-market paperback of the poetry he wrote about life on the mean streets. One afternoon I was walking up Yonge approaching Gerrard when I saw Hans standing on the corner outside Bassel's Restaurant. He was wearing an electric blue shirt with enormous white polka dots, a vest made of some rough fibrous material resembling a welcome mat, and wide-cord bell-bottom trousers held up by a four-inch-high belt with an enormous silver buckle. I started to say hello, but he shushed me. "Can't talk," he said *sotto voce*. "I'm in plain clothes."

Getting a more serious collection of poetry published entailed more difficulty. Ramsay Derry had left Macmillan of Canada after a tussle and been replaced by his friend Douglas Gibson, who had been brought in from Doubleday, a couple of blocks up Bond Street. The result was a publishing melodrama during which I had the poor timing to submit my next poetry manuscript to Macmillan, which rejected it at once. The collection was a vast improvement on *Our Man in Utopia*, for I think I had begun to find my own voice—weary, urban, edgy perhaps, often supplicatory. Later, I sent the manuscript to Michael Macklem of Oberon Press in Ottawa, which was then one of the most fecund small publishers. Macklem, who used to drive personally across Canada each year selling books from the back of his van and in that way stay in touch with the bookselling community, wrote to indicate that he would surely want to publish it. He went on to say that he first had to run it by David Helwig for his opinion. Then suddenly the typescript came back, crumpled and postage-due, and with no letter to explain the *volte-face*. The book was finally rescued for publication by a figure from my Anansi past, Dave Godfrey, who since breaking with Dennis Lee had already founded two other publishing houses: new press, which had just been taken over by the Stoddart publishing family, and Press Porcépic, which, miraculously, sold through two printings of my poems. The satisfaction of knowing that it had gone back to press was my best and almost my only compensation, for by the end of 1975, the year following publication, I received a royalty statement for $67.20 on second-printing sales. I know because I have my financial files and also my journals for that pivotal year in history—the year when Saigon fell and the year when deficit financing finally caught up with *Saturday Night*.

# CHAPTER TWO

# The Decline
## of Toronto
# the Good

IN THE LATE 1960s there was a famous American photograph (you saw it reproduced everywhere) of Huey Newton, the leader of the militant Black Panther Party, sitting in a large and enormously high-backed wicker chair. In the 1970s Yousuf Karsh's photograph of Margaret Atwood posing on an almost identical piece of furniture seemed almost as ubiquitous in Canada. I doubt that Karsh ever noticed the similarity, but many others felt it somehow. Peggy Atwood was *our* Huey Newton; cultural nationalism and feminism were Canada's Black Power movement. She also may have been Bob Fulford's only repeated failure as a subject of journalistic investigation. He kept writing and writing about her, articles, reviews, essays, columns, trying to account for her importance, which of course he recognized without quite being able to explain. Finally she grew exasperated and caricatured him in a piece of fiction. It was sometimes a bit dodgy trying to be friends with both of them.

Such is one image I call up from the limbo of the decade in-between. What else is stored there? Let me see. Two of the most important institutions on CBC Radio began in the 1970s, *As It Happens* in 1971 and *Sunday Morning* in 1976. In 1973 the Longhouse, Toronto's all-Canadiana bookstore, opened its doors, and Ontario called a Royal commission to investigate American influence in book publishing (and found it all pervasive). At the same time, the Toronto media were titillated almost beyond endurance by the immigration to their city of Xaviera Hollander, a famous madam, known as the Happy Hooker, who had quit New York after the Knapp Commission inquiring into police corruption, the panel that was bound up with the Serpico case of the same period. Also in 1973, to further anchor Canadian events in an international context, Bernie Cornfeld, the Turkish-born former Brooklyn cab driver, went to jail in Switzerland following the collapse of his multi-billion-dollar mutual fund empire, Investors Overseas Services. The following year, 1974, the federal government opened Harbourfront in Toronto and, in an unrelated matter, Peter Demeter was convicted of hiring someone to kill his wife. The latter was a story that became the subject of one of the few really first-rate Canadian true-crime books, *By Persons Unknown*, published in 1977 by my friend George Jonas and his wife, Barbara Amiel (who later married Conrad Black).

Or take 1975, as the median point of the decade. As I recall 1975, there was still some of the sixties in the air, though we who had survived that time were starting to grow concerned, ever so privately, about the way our youth was vanishing in a vapour. Everyone I knew in the Annex belonged to the Karma Co-op, a bulk-food enterprise, and still listened to Jungle Jay Nelson on CHUM, home of what were being called oldies but didn't yet seem that way to those of us who had sung along with them when they were new. People still attended the Mariposa Folk Festival and went to the Colonial on Yonge Street to hear jazz. You couldn't mistake the fact that the demographic make-up of the city was changing day by day; many of us read *Contrast*, the important African-Canadian newspaper of the time. We knew the difference between sound judgement and poor taste. Everyone had instant contempt for one of the year's hit songs, "Feelings" as recorded by Morris Albert (though written by Louis Gaste, who had composed "How Much Is That Doggie in the Window?" a generation earlier).

In ways that didn't appear logical but felt coherent at the time, events such as some of the ones I pick almost at random seemed to be the cruel seventies finally asserting themselves over the gentler and more deluded sixties for which some people were feeling premature nostalgia. Looking back, though, I sense that while the two styles of public existence were sort of blended into one style culturally, there was an event in 1970 so conspicuous that it appeared even then to set the tone for what lay ahead. I refer to the conscious destruction of downtown Toronto by the Eaton family.

The 1970s was the decade in which Toronto discovered greed on the heroic American scale. Property development was the way to quick money and a guarantee of shady politics. A reform movement sprang up in municipal government as street after street of lovely Victorian buildings, both commercial and residential, were pulled down in Toronto's headlong rush towards Americanism in all things, the visible ones most of all. Only once did I actually meet a developer—one of the mightiest—but at the time that trouble came to *Saturday Night* I was working hard on a piece that dealt, in its way, with the consequences of the Eaton Centre, for which the department store dynasty had caused entire blocks of Yonge Street to be razed.

A much-loved figure on the fringes of the local arts scene in those days was Gerald Lampert (whose memory is preserved in the name of an annual literary award). He was part of the old Spadina Avenue, when *Spadina*, now synonymous with transplanted Hong-kong bustle, instead conjured up images of the rag trade and downtown Jewish culture. The Avenue, as old-timers called it, was where the Yiddish theatres had been. In the middle 1970s, before the GATT started to squeeze the small Canadian manufacturers out of the marketplace, lower Spadina was still home to much of the garment business. This umbrella term included not only factories large and small but also such peripheral enterprises as the shop of the hatter Sammy Taft, who had once made snap-brim fedoras for international show-biz names, prominent members of Detroit's Purple Gang and others who considered themselves the very indices of fashion. Spadina still had the best delicatessens, too. It also had the old

Labour Lyceum, where Emma Goldman had lain in state in 1940 when death stopped that great heart of hers during her final exile.

Gerry Lampert was a small round middle-aged man who chain-smoked pipe tobacco and had worked for years in advertising and public relations but had really wanted to be a novelist and live the literary life. He went through the motions of running his own creative shop out of the old bank building on the northeast corner of Queen and Spadina, a structure that really needed its collar and cuffs turned, being full of other one- and two-person businesses frayed with the same promise of failure as Lampert Advertising. But Gerry's look of professional underachievement belied an entrepreneur of Canadian culture and a novelist whose two books, though forgotten now, were well received and widely read in their time. I think that I helped in some small way to get one of them published. In return, he showed me the tricks of being a book packager: someone who sells an editorial idea to a publisher and subcontracts out the writing, design and production of the title, supplying the publisher with finished books bearing the publisher's imprint. This was an art at which many people were claiming to be adepts. Gerry also did a little teaching and founded what I believe was the first of the city's annual writing workshops. Aspiring poets and fiction-writers would pay to stay for a couple of weeks in University of Toronto dormitories while attending the classes, lectures and readings Gerry had organized, featuring professionals in the various writing disciplines. The scale was small but the idea was a fresh one in those days. Most of Gerry's ad hoc faculty were Canadians, such as John Herbert (real name: John Brundage), author of *Fortune in Men's Eyes*, a play about homosexual rape in prison. The work was Herbert's only hit but a huge one indeed. That success and acclaim lay some years behind him when Herbert stopped me walking down Spadina and introduced himself rather dramatically as a fellow faculty member for the week. Then, without preamble, he proceeded to list all the productions of *Fortune* round the world, how much they had taken in at the box office and what the critics had said in praise of his genius. Another faculty recidivist was Austin Clarke, the novelist, story-writer and sometime Barbadian diplomat, a pioneering Black voice in contemporary Canadian literature, whom I liked ever since he had run for mayor of Toronto a few years earlier (a campaign I had an assignment to cover for the *Village Voice*, until, early on, Austin tossed his hat back out of the ring). A foreign visitor who came up for the workshop every year was Alice Denham, the author of two sexy novels, *My Darling from the Lions* and *Amo*, which seemed, in those more innocent times, to be breakthrough feminist erotica but were actually, as I look back, just the usual male soft-porn told in a female voice. Even if that were not the case, I don't think later feminists would have welcomed her into the canon, for Alice had been one of the early *Playboy* centrefolds (in 1955, though it wasn't considered polite to pinpoint the year in her hearing). Alice, who hailed from Florida originally, maintained an enormous cataract of red hair and addressed everybody she met as *Honey*. To supplement her writing income, she was a building super in Greenwich Village. She also conducted an English literature survey course for New York cops at night-school. "Once you've taught Wordsworth to policemen," she would say, "you can teach anybody anything," as events, I suppose, were proving.

I was up in Gerry's office one day (he allowed me photocopying privileges in return for minor jobs of proofreading) when he told me that he wanted to talk to me. He had a *very* important businessman coming in to see him about some PR work and there would be good money in it for both of us. I hung around, as instructed, but hung *back*, just within earshot, when the air was suddenly made serious by the arrival of Paul Reichmann, the president of the city's biggest high-rise developer, Olympia & York, the mastermind behind such transforming structures as First Canadian Place (and, in later years, the Canary Wharf project, the biggest in Britain, which bankrupted them for a time). Reichmann and his brothers, Ralph and Albert, were often spoken about but seldom seen, except in the standard promotional portraits, which is how I recognized him instantly. This trio, who had fled Europe via North Africa with the rest of their family after the Second World War, were already Canada's biggest landlords. But their strongest renown was for how closely knit and devout they were, standing out, when they did venture into public view, by their Orthodox dress and beards and the extremity of their rectitude and grim politeness. How Gerry got an audience with the Reichmanns was a mystery to me. So was how he got the Reichmanns to come to *him*, with the head of the concern favouring him with a climb up the dusty stairs to the noticeably unprepossessing home of Lampert Advertising—the kind of office where there always seem to be cats asleep on piles of sedentary invoices.

Eavesdropping on their conversation (difficult, because Reichmann was so soft-spoken), I picked up the fact that Gerry had somehow got word to them through intermediaries. His message was that he thought it unfair of them to give all their hundreds of thousands of dollars worth of PR and advertising to the major agencies in town when there were Jewish small business people such as himself who were just getting by. Reichmann had a new structure going up somewhere on King Street and gave Gerry a verbal contract to get some press attention for it. I must have been slack-jawed when Reichmann left, for Gerry was careful to swear me to secrecy. Since I had friends at all the newspapers, Gerry promised me $500 to see if I could get one of them to run a photograph of the building site under one pretext or another. I was of two minds about letting myself be co-opted by PR work but took the money, because Canada was undergoing one of its more gruelling postal strikes at the time and my finances were even more perilous than usual. In fact, my main income at that moment came from writing for Ross McLean, the former *enfant terrible* and boy genius of CBC radio and television, whose arch personality always got in the way of his career advancement and, after a certain point, put it in reverse. Ross was now reduced to being station manager of CBLT, the local O-and-O, and he was paying me $49.50 a week on a short writing contract. I didn't have a lot of trouble getting one of the papers to run a picture of the construction cranes atop the Olympia & York site, accompanied by a one-inch cutline. Gerry duly gave me the equivalent of ten weeks' income. I can't imagine how much he charged Reichmann when he sent him the clipping along with his bill. In such ways as these did important people sometimes patronize the arts without knowing it.

I am able to quote these pathetic little sums of mine with exactitude not because acid has etched them on my memory but rather because I can refer to my old financial log. I have my journal, too. Looking back over it now for the first time in twenty years, I squirm at the abundant evidence of my immaturity (how slow to grow, how quick to decay). But I also find it useful for recapturing transient events and fleeting moods.

Fulford, at home with the ague, calls late this morning, inviting me up for a chat. The housekeeper brings tea to the split-level den while we talk 3 ½ hours about the state of *Saturday Night* and about writing, etc. Bob has become a good friend these past two or three years especially. As a result, there is some uneasiness in his discussions of business matters with me. But this is more than made up for by the frankness and conviviality of talk on other issues. Says Bob at one point: "I think a journalist in this country should be able to make as much money as any other professional. I can, but I have to do so many different things—really keeps me busy, and then I only make as much as an ordinary lawyer." I read these comments into the record as being completely out-of-character. Bob's always almost self-effacing and seemingly unconcerned with monetary matters, except where *Saturday Night* itself is concerned. Then he frets and agonizes.

For a permanent plank in the editor's job at *Saturday Night* was helping to keep the place supplied with investment fodder, as supporters, once dragged into the morass of the magazine's finances, were quick to struggle out again. The behind-the-scenes waxing and waning were naturally reflected in the magazine itself, which for one humiliating period had to be printed on paper not much better than newsprint and, for one memorable issue, shrank to a mere twenty-eight pages.

By this time, *Saturday Night* had moved far away from the Oom-pah-pah Room and was occupying the upper floor of a small nondescript building on the north side of St Clair Avenue, a few blocks east of Yonge. The office was tiny, perhaps only 1,000 square feet, but even at that it proved too large, so the magazine sublet the front couple of rooms to a minor insurance company, Abstainers', whose policy-holders were all non-smoking teetotallers. One had to push one's way through the strait-laced tenants to reach the actual leaseholder's more depraved atmosphere. Through the early months of 1974, I was going there frequently for pep talks and strategy sessions with Bob about a piece I was working on for him. Or sometimes we would lunch at a place up the street where we were bound to meet Gordon Sinclair, the ancient broadcaster and long-time Toronto *Star* reporter (who once told me how the *Star* flew him to Chicago in a chartered plane to cover the aftermath of the St Valentine's Day Massacre in 1929). "You're puttin' out a pretty good book there, Bob," Sinclair would always say about *Saturday Night*.

Yonge had supplanted King as Toronto's main shopping thoroughfare about eighty years earlier and was a wonderfully Canadian street, all of a piece but so arranged that its character changed every few blocks, as though cloud formations racing overhead were first masking the sunlight, then letting it shine through. One short stretch, for example, contained both an all-night drug store that was a sort of union hiring-hall for streetwalkers as well as the evangelical mission whose huge neon cross flashed JESUS SAVES in orange letters (a sign that used to attract filmmakers like moths). By walking just a few blocks south, you were in the old financial district, with close ranks of early skyscrapers belonging to the old-line companies such as Canadian Pacific, their architectural beauty not completely obscured by so many decades of city grime. This area also had numerous small retail businesses that had been in the same location forever. One tailor shop, for instance, specialized in the military, and was the only place in town sanctioned to renew the ribbons on orders and decorations and to supply the miniatures, in tin, that certain formal invitations used to call for discreetly in the lower left-hand corner. The shopkeeper once showed me that he stocked medals and ribbons from the Korean War back through those given to participants in the North-West Rebellion of 1885. "But surely anyone entitled to wear a medal from the days of Riel is dead now," I said. He gave me a look like the one that tailor at Gieves in London must have given Charles Laughton: one never knows, sir, does one?

By pulling down a big piece of Yonge Street and substituting a huge mall and galleria, the Eatons not only disrupted the traditional street grid but also took out a lot of these old firms. With something vital now missing, the street grew weak and ripe for infection. Within a few years, the old Yonge Street strip, so called, with its dirty-book stores and dildo shops, had taken on an air of quaintness as a new type of business, massage parlours, spread all up and down that and adjacent streets. I was curious about this phenomenon. Who was behind it? Was it as easy to make money as it looked? Was it a good or bad development for the traditional prostitutes? What did it say about independent female entrepreneurs? (for this burgeoning new sex trade seemed to have bypassed the old pimp system, though a good deal of exploitation remained, even in the many establishments ostensibly run by women). This was what I was working on for *Saturday Night*. The assignment threw me into contact with many improbable but nonetheless genuine characters.

One of them was a Ukrainian-Canadian who encouraged people to call him Eddie Chicago. He lived in one room of a spacious office suite overlooking Yonge, where his colleagues sometimes gathered. A

In 1970 "one could live quite well in London, even if officially poor.
In those days, it was not even expensive to pop over to Paris to hang
out at such places as George Whitman's Shakespeare & Company,
the English-language bookshop that claimed direct descent
from Sylvia Beach's . . ." *(Courtesy of the Thomas Fisher
Rare Book Library, University of Toronto)*

A rare dual portrait of two literary antagonists: Kildare Dobbs, the urbane Irish-Canadian *litterateur*, and Hugh Garner, the author of *Cabbagetown*, whom *Maclean's* once called "Canada's best-known drunk since Sir John A. Macdonald." *(Courtesy of Arlene Lampert)*

"Austin Clarke, the novelist, short-story writer and sometime Barbadian diplomat, a pioneering Black voice in Canadian literature, whom I liked ever since he had run for mayor of Toronto a few years earlier. . . ." *(Courtesy of Arlene Lampert)*

To Doug Fetherling
dear friend
Bob Fulford
July 27/75

Robert Fulford, the editor of *Saturday Night* throughout
the decade (and then some): "six feet tall and fleshy, with an
enormous oval face full of kindness and curiosity." *(Courtesy
of the Thomas Fisher Rare Book Library, University of Toronto)*

Margaret Atwood's rise to prominence, to the point where she became the Canadian author with the widest international reputation,
was one of the key phenomena of seventies culture. Trying to maintain friendships with both her and Fulford could be "a bit dodgey
at times." *(Photograph by Oliver Cogswell. Courtesy of the photographer
and the Thomas Fisher Rare Book Library, University of Toronto)*

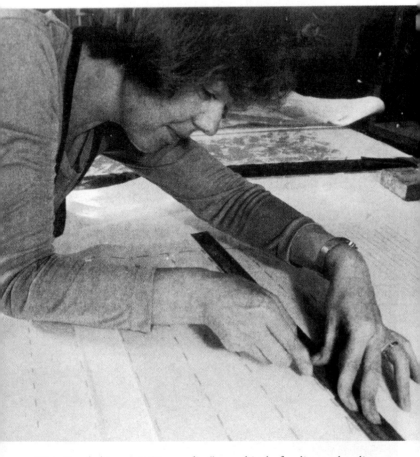

Vera Frenkel in 1976. Her studio "was a kind of unlicensed atelier with many of the attributes of a speakeasy." *(Courtesy of Vera Frenkel)*

The author in a still from Vera Frenkel's 1976 video *Signs of a Plot: A Text, a True Story & a Work of Art.* "I appeared in the role of a cynical journalist; I believe she chose me because I already owned the most important prop, a nicely battered fedora. . . ." *(Courtesy of Vera Frenkel)*

The author, looking appropriately exhausted, as the decade drew to a close. "For a dozen years I never knew the luxury of an unexpressed thought." *(Courtesy of the Thomas Fisher Rare Book Library, University of Toronto)*

beautiful expanse of desk, a fine old thing with the silhouette of an ocean liner though made of wood (mahogany, I think, or possibly teak), was one of its main features. Another was a macaw that stood on its perch in one of the dimly lit corners and every now and then broke squelch with the words, "Bawk! Who's the pretty boy, then? Who's the pretty boy? Baaawwk." Eddie was apparently fond of a 1953 Clark Gable–Susan Hayward film called *Soldier of Fortune* in which Gable is some sort of wealthy rogue living in a penthouse overlooking Hongkong Harbour and sometimes plays a phonograph record of Chicago traffic noises to remind himself of the place to which, for reasons implied but not explained, he can never return. Eddie had a tape of honking horns, blowing whistles and screaming cabbies. He would play it to suggest a similar picturesque misstep somewhere in his own background. Personally, I never believed him.

I got to know Eddie through a guy named McElroy, who spent much of his time in a poker game that originally rotated between Rochdale College and the old King Edward Hotel, which had yet to be restored to its original glory. Indeed, the King Eddy had turned its entire mezzanine over to wholesalers of cheap clothing and its lobby to hustlers and dosers. McElroy was, I'm sure, a good poker player, but he always had cash-flow problems, and so one time when he was on a winning streak he bought several points in a little bookstore. In McElroy, Eddie smelled a potential investor. But then the only books Eddie read came wrapped in cellophane and cost five dollars for thirty-two pages.

"What I think you should do is branch out," Eddie said one day, coming to the point at length. "Diversification is the key to modern business." Eddie uttered this as though quoting from something he had read in a dentist's office. "It so happens that I'm hunting a partner in a new enterprise. Why not come take a look around?"

McElroy (as he related the encounter to me in a later interview) was rightly dubious but oddly intrigued. The two of them jostled their way up Yonge Street, which the city elders had decided to close to vehicular traffic each summer as a sort of make-work project for beggars and dips. They had to sidestep aggressive members of several religious sects, some police, some tourists from the suburbs and some adolescents giving out handbills for massage parlours. Eddie Chicago asked one of the handbill people how it was going, then dragged McElroy sharply through a doorway and up a flight of stairs.

It was only at that point (he would tell me) that McElroy realized that what his friend was running was a sleazy massage parlour. When McElroy exclaimed this, Eddie corrected him. "We can't call them massage parlours. Massages are given by people licensed under the Drugless Practitioners' Act. What this is, is a body-rub parlour, which we like to call a health club." At the top of the steps was a buzzer. This device represented a considerable capital expenditure for someone in that business, or so McElroy confided to me later, after he had begun researching the potential investment.

McElroy, my old notes tell me, learned from

friends of the anti-body-rub faction at City Hall that there were eighty-one such establishments in Toronto, but he swore that there must have been a lot more, for in the interest of informing himself he had decided to scout as many of them as he could, to learn the mechanics and finances of the business before getting back to Eddie with his decision. Eddie's, he quickly learned, was a middle-of-the-road operation in every way except location, which was better than most. It was a perfect set-up, and he wondered that Eddie should want a partner to split the profit.

During the next few weeks McElroy went to body-rub parlours up and down Yonge, on side-streets, in outlying boroughs; to others in private houses, over stores or attached to strip-joints and X-rated cinemas. Many of them had no extras of any kind. He had so many body rubs he was in danger of getting skin cancer from the friction, but this wasn't what worried him. What worried him was what his accountant would say if he were to ask advice about investing in such a scheme. When he was beginning to get into gambling heavily, McElroy had decided that he needed an accountant to help keep him straight with Revenue Canada. At the suggestion of one of the executives he was cheating at poker, he came to know a fancy North Toronto accountant. The accountant had saved him a great deal of money over the months, and no doubt prevented brushes with Ottawa. He was an upper-middle-class accountant accustomed to dealing with vast amounts of other people's honest wealth, and he came to regard McElroy with a vicarious awe yet with an almost paternal benevolence.

While getting rubbed all over the metropolitan area, McElroy (as he told it) would lie there looking at the mirrored ceilings, worrying. Would his accountant ridicule him for wanting to put money into such a venture? Would he laugh and scold as he had done when McElroy sought advice about a young Italian-Canadian middleweight he'd once thought of helping to back? The opportunity to join the syndicate forming to promote the fighter came to him, like everything in McElroy's life, from the poker table. A better card-player than his well-off marks, he was less the business person. He'd gone to the accountant to ask if he could claim depreciation every time the fighter got his jaw broken by some ringer from Winnipeg. The fatherly CA had laughed at such ignorance of the tax codes. It had been humiliating.

As he made his rounds, McElroy carried a little note pad, which he let me see once, in which he wrote down what he observed about the body-rub parlours. For example, he noted that several of the downtown establishments had the same unusual (and horrid) wallpaper as Eddie Chicago's place. It worried him that this could not be just a deadly decorative coincidence. Surely, given a choice, no one would deliberately re-do a place of business in this absurd shade and pattern. It must be that several of the parlours were owned by the same people and were fitted out at the same time. Perhaps by G——, who was living in the Caribbean now but still owned many of the porno bookstores. G—— was reportedly not a person with whom to interfere. "Not organized crime exactly," McElroy told me on the record, "but no computer analyst either." He wondered why anyone would compete against himself in this way.

It was a business, he discovered, in which everyone tried to come up with something a little different. There was one place that for $40 offered a one-hour "combination," meaning that the masseuse would get into the shower with you. Across the street was another where the same phrase meant that one was rubbed by the masseuse for half an hour and then one rubbed *her* for the same length of time. McElroy let me quote him as reporting that this latter was not nearly so enjoyable.

There were other things too. Of course there were saunas, movies, body-painting and nude photography ($30 and up for eight Polaroids, which one could keep), all of which was old hat. Other places offered two attendants to work on you instead of one, or male attendants for the gay trade. At still other establishments, the *specialité* might be private striptease, nude dancing, nude encounter sessions ($20 for twenty minutes) or nude card games. At the last of these, McElroy, who tried all this in the interest of market research, naturally excelled. At this stage, he said, he was excited about the business prospects, the limitless potential for exploitation. "It seemed," he told me enthusiastically, "like the biggest rip-off since the comet Kahoutek."

McElroy one day discovered a spot advertising geisha baths and an "escort service"—a phrase then brand-new to Toronto. But when he went in to ask about these blandishments, the man behind the front counter told him a sad story. "I just took over this place a couple of months ago," he said, "and I haven't had time to change the sign yet. I don't have none of that stuff you ask about." The fellow added, "I'm sorry I ever got into this business," and McElroy besought him to elaborate. "Well," the man replied, "first there's the shortage of girls. I was giving them thirty per cent of each customer but they kept going to work other places. So I raised the split to fifty/fifty. This is to keep them from giving extras on the side. You see, if they give extras—in my place at least—it's all their own doing. They keep it all for themselves. But I want to run a clean place, you understand?, because I don't want no trouble with the cops. They've started smashing down doors around Eglinton and up north, and I think this is meant as a warning to the rest of us, downtown."

What had the so-called escort service been when it existed? McElroy still wanted to know.

"That was where you could hire the girl to take to your own place, but the cops must have come down on the owner. This is what I've been trying to tell you. This address is on their books now. I got a $1,200 sauna cabinet sitting out back that I can't install because the city is hassling me about zoning, saying this one building, between all these stores and everything, is residential. Can you believe it?"

McElroy learned later that another problem of the body-rub shops was that they had no place to advertise. When the first ones opened in Toronto about 1972, they were careful to be private clubs, issuing membership cards to their customers and making certain no one broke the no-hanky-panky rules printed on the backs. They advertised in the classified sections of two of the three daily newspapers (the *Globe and Mail* then limiting itself to ads from registered masseurs and masseuses who operated by appointment). But later the *Star* began rejecting their ads, some believed at the suggestion of the vice squad. For a long while only the *Sun*, the still-new rightist tabloid, would carry the ads, and it had a virtual monopoly that sometimes ran to a profitable two full columns a day. Then, mysteriously, the *Sun* also began refusing such ads. To relieve the vacuum, one clever operator hired a registered masseuse to act as a front for the purpose of advertising, while also having employees who gave rubs and made no bones about their extras. For good measure, this person added an entirely new service: nude hairstyling.

Faced with this quiet discrimination, as well as with municipal attempts to have the province drive them out of business altogether, some of the Yonge Street owners got together and started a publication of their own as a platform for their opinions on civil liberties and coincidentally a medium for advertising. It was short-lived, and no one quite knew what had happened to it. Later, the proprietor of an out-of-the-way parlour founded a ratty-looking sheet purporting to be a guide to Toronto dining and nightlife but which was mostly body-rub ads. Lacking even the half-serious intent of its predecessor, it did little to help the industry or clear the name of its sponsoring establishments. They had come under increasing fire from typically moralistic Ontario editorialists.

The last time I saw McElroy I was walking past his

bookstore when he ran outside to tell me this story. On his arm was Tina, a young woman from Macao who appeared to be equal parts Chinese, Portuguese and Black, and looked somewhat naked even with all her clothes on. McElroy informed me that he had decided to turn down Eddie's offer after meeting Tina in a body-rub shop where she'd gone to work after dropping out of some fringe religious group. She beamed at him while he told me how once he'd gone into her place he couldn't keep himself away. The mutual attraction had been too great. His gambling had begun to suffer. His research, to which variety was essential, also fell to ruin. The relationship had begun as the chatty kind a person often has with a rubber, he said, making it sound like the modern equivalent of the traditional customer–barber arrangement. At length, he confided to me, as Tina continued to smile broadly, they found themselves alone *in puris naturalibus* and events took their course. His devotion to her, as he told me, had helped her to recover her lost spiritual ideals and make them contagious, to the point where they were now burning the joss at both ends and planning to go into business as a team.

"What we intend to do," he told me, "is something entirely new for Toronto. Nude worship. Tina's going to be the priestess and me the acolyte and business manager. Lonely sinners can join for a few dollars and for a few more get the laying on of hands, nude confessionals, that type of thing. It's a natural. Besides, I'm hoping that once we get incorporated as a religious body, the cops won't dare bother us. Sanctity of the cathedral, separation of church and state, and all like that."

The above, along with a dozen other related characters almost equally strange, had the ingredients of a wonderful magazine article of a type then fashionable, in which the hapless writer's description of the search for the yarn was itself an integral part of the bigger story. I had finished, Bob had edited it, and it was to appear in the September 1974 issue. This was the *Saturday Night* that never appeared. The funds had run out, the wobbly superstructure had collapsed at last; there was no money for the printer. The various media were full of obituaries, but Bob remained in the office at the back of Abstainers' Insurance. *Saturday Night* was beyond the point of needing angels to give more money. It needed an entrepreneur—a real one, not some Eddie Chicago—to come and reinvent it. Meanwhile, my piece gradually grew dated and then useless, for the nature of the sex trade in Toronto was about to change. A twelve-year-old Portuguese shoeshine boy was found brutally murdered on the roof of one of the Yonge Street parlours. The killing had nothing to do with the business below but was the work of three pedophiles who got life sentences. The police, however, used the crime as an excuse to drive the body-rub places out of business—only later, in February 1981, to deal with the gay community as well, by a mammoth concerted raid on the steam baths involving two hundred cops and resulting in three hundred arrests. This was a period when public attitudes had raced ahead of the police department's. Toronto in the 1970s, for

instance, is regarded as a kind of golden age of indige-
nous live theatre, what with the Tarragon, Theatre
Passe Muraille, Factory Theatre Lab and other companies that had their beginnings then, letting the
audience get to know a new world of wonderful
actors (I think of them as the Clare Coulter generation) and playwrights as different as Rick Salutin,
David French and Carol Bolt. Yet when I look back
on this time, what I recall most vividly is being in the
audience when, at just about the same time as the *Saturday Night* debacle, the cops, citing nudity and
obscenity on stage, raided a performance at Passe
Muraille. The production was called *I Love You, Baby
Blue*, a spoof of Toronto's sexual mores; the title was a
reference to the most popular feature on CITY television, the station recently cofounded by Moses
Znaimer, a style-setting entrepreneur in what now
seems to have been that decade of entrepreneurs. In
any event, after the early 1970s not just Yonge Street
but Toronto in general got progressively uglier, less
tolerant and certainly more violent. The same Eaton
Centre that had seemed such an architectural and
city-planning tragedy became not only Toronto's
most popular tourist attraction but also the scene of
attacks by youth gangs and other violence—to the
point where the police had to open a miniature station right inside the door. All that saved Toronto was
that immigration was virtually doubling its popula-
tion, to the point where the cops would find it necessary to advertise that they had staff on hand or on call
who could speak a total of 140 different languages and
dialects. It was during this period, I believe, that

Toronto achieved the remarkable feat of becoming the world's most cosmopolitan big city while remaining one of the least sophisticated. And people said we couldn't have it both ways.

———————

When Rachel walked out on me, I slid once more under the waves of depression. You could say that the pattern itself was becoming depressingly familiar. At times the water was cold and dark and visibility almost nil. Yet after a number of months, I began to enjoy the thought of living on my own. Well, not on my own exactly, for after a while I moved out of the apartment we had shared and took up a small space in a communal house a few doors down Howland Avenue: a congenial place, full of perennial graduate students, visiting Australians, and the like. The house was one of those large comfortable Annex structures with wainscots and a stained-glass window on the first-floor landing. It was owned by the mother of one of the residents, Susan Hammond, a piano teacher who later made a career of producing and performing on a popular series of audiotapes that made classical music accessible to the very young. Everyone at the house welcomed me—and Heywood, the dog, who became a pet with many communal masters and mistresses. This allowed me to slip away to England and other places, knowing that she was in loving hands. For these were busy times, the middle to late 1970s, when I finally came into demand at the magazines, newspapers and book publishers and was always, depending on the moment, either the bright star or a hunted rogue. This became my much-delayed bachelor period as well, and I spent a lot of time with friends who were either single or between marriages or nearly so.

One such acquaintance was John Fraser, about five years older than me, who was then still dating but was not yet married to Elizabeth MacCallum, the granddaughter of the Group of Seven's patron. His own grandfather had been one of the founders of Dominion Securities (whereas his step-mother, who continued to hold the record for the number of appearances on the cover of *Vogue* or *Harper's Bazaar*, once had been unsuccessfully engaged to marry Howard Hughes—she remembered that he was stone deaf, at a point long before the Hughes biographies attest to this fact). In Upper Canada (and in anglo Lower Canada too), status was still often a matter of how accomplished one's grandparents had been, quite separate from the question of how much money had survived (usually none). There were young people running about dying for the opportunity to tell you casually how their grandfather had been an important politician or man of business or, in one familiar case, a baronet.

As for John Fraser, I had seen him briefly at the old *Telegram* before it closed in 1971, and he was now the dance critic of the *Globe and Mail*. He was a short not-yet-pudgy individual with black hair and matching glasses. He always wore a bow-tie. I have come to believe that this last fact was somehow bound up with a desire to embargo the Windsor knot as a monarchist's silent, unforgiving protest against Wallis Simpson and the attendant Abdication Crisis of 1936. *Silent* seems an odd word to apply here, for John's most noticeable personal characteristic was that he loved to talk. Some would call him the city's leading gossip, but I feel that this title was merely the incidental by-product of his truly heroic verbal stamina. In all the years I knew him I cannot recall him pausing for breath, much less assuming the posture of an attentive listener. I remember meeting him after work one winter afternoon at the bar of the Sheraton Centre, opposite New City Hall. Before I could take my seat he began to update me on some long, complicated scandal that was unfolding somewhere, and he talked for two hours straight. He was still at it when we went down to the lobby to find a taxi to take the two of us to our respective homes. In fact, he didn't even pause when we had to pass, in separate cubicles, through the revolving doors. As luck would have it, this was the exact moment when he revealed the killer's identity, so to speak. Refusing to acknowledge my signals that the continuity of the narrative had been broken, he carried on without let-up until the cab arrived at my place and I hopped out. I could see him still bombarding the ears of the driver, a non-English-speaker, as the taxi pulled away in the snowy evening.

I found the barrage of language oddly comforting, especially on days when my stutter was acting up, as I wasn't being called on to finish the sentences I'd begun or in fact to keep up my end of the conversation at all. Once, years later, after John and Elizabeth had two daughters, I had to call after dinner at their house in the eastern Annex on some urgent media matter. Elizabeth was out for the evening and John was supposedly watching over the two little girls, who were having what sounded like an extended pillow fight upstairs. John excused himself, went to the bottom of the steps and yelled up to their bedroom: "If you two don't settle down, I'm going to send Mr Fetherling up there to *try* to read you a story." Silence descended like a leaded curtain.

The *Globe* of those days, where I had many friendly acquaintances and only one or two in the opposite camp, was in a grand period. The editor was Richard J. Doyle, known as Dic, who wore his spectacles on a black cord suspended around his neck and had remarkable gifts of leadership. He was the sort of editor who liked skilled writers ("feisty" ones, as he described them). He was also, on another level, prone to employ the handsome male offspring of old Bourbon families, all of whom had either gone to Queen's or looked as though they had. He was mild-mannered and soft-spoken but was made of strong material. He was given to bouts of investigative fever, some of which, such as a long series on police brutality, actually benefited the community. Others are more blurry in my mind and probably in their effectiveness. What was that long business about picking on the Children's Aid Society, of all people? And what was that vile racist scare about Rastafarians? Or another about Marxists having infiltrated the post office?

No matter. Doyle radiated the suggestion that he would always go to the wall for his people if they were in the right. His managing editor was the more classically tough-talking Clark Davey, like Doyle, a native of Chatham, Ontario. They made quite a team: sweet and sour. In a movie about the *Globe* of this period, they would have been played by William Holden and Lee Marvin respectively.

Doyle was the kind of person you wanted to work for if you believed, as I did, that you were a writer trapped in the role of the journalist, or if you held that the profession was somewhat self-limiting and only weakly magnetized. He knew that I felt this way, and once tried to find a staff position for me in the arts section, where I was already freelancing enough to enjoy a cousin's status at the family table. The truth was, there were no vacancies in the foreseeable future, but he very kindly offered me a way in, with a new beat of his own creation, covering the Royal Ontario Museum and other "institutions." The word *institutions* may have frightened me. So did the prospect of an untried job description whose mandate was open to differing interpretations all up and down the whole editorial hierarchy, which included the two people there who, I knew, wished to ambush me. Reluctantly, I turned it down—softly, I hoped. But in the process I inadvertently and with the greatest unwillingness miffed Doyle. So I was fated never to work for the *Globe and Mail*, which doesn't knock twice and which, in any event, would stop drawing people from all political philosophies once Doyle, to the surprise of many and the disappointment of more, accepted a summons to the Senate from, of all people, Brian Mulroney.

One of Doyle's outlandish and most obviously successful ideas was to send my friend Fraser, by now the drama critic, to Beijing. This was in 1977, when the *Globe*, which had been the first western paper with a bureau there after the communist revolution, was still one of only a small handful so situated. The American press had no resident reporters until 1979, for example. This meant that the *Globe* dispatches were printed in other English-language papers round the world. Mao had died and China was poised to enter some new period, no one knew quite what.

Envious people found absurd the idea of sending this hyper-loquacious arts type with impeccable Anglo-Canadian establishment connections to cover Chinese affairs. In fact, though, the decision turned out advantageously. Fraser had a natural talent for the necessary intrigue. When he was dance critic, he had aided in Mikhail Baryshnikov's defection while the Bolshoi was performing in Canada. But he had never before had cause to imagine anything like China, where he became involved in the Democracy Wall protests in 1978 and knew the pro-democracy agitator Wei Jingsheng, later imprisoned. Fraser's experiences there affected his life profoundly, as I believe was probably true for the other *Globe* correspondents before him, most of whom I knew.

One of them, Charles Taylor, was among the people I saw most often and most enjoyed. As strangers never seemed to tire of pointing out in whispers, Charles was the son of E.P. Taylor, the favourite capitalist of Canadian editorial writers and cartoonists throughout the 1940s and 1950s. It had once been considered clever to say that *E.P.* stood for Excess Profits, a reference to the country's excess-profits tax during the Second World War. In fact, Taylor had served as one of C.D. Howe's dollar-a-year men, a kind of brains trust of the best financial minds and entrepreneurs assisting the federal government with the quick transition to a martial economy. Taylor and Roy Thomson once crossed the North Atlantic on a corvette despite threats by Lord Haw Haw, the Nazi radio propagandist, that they would be torpedoed. But it was only after the war that E.P. became so ubiquitous. He controlled half the supermarkets, he developed Don Mills as the country's first fully planned suburb, he rationalized the breweries first in Canada and then in Britain and he turned Lyford Cay in the Bahamas into an offshore tax haven for heliotropic millionaires like himself. Many will remember photographs of him standing in the winner's circle after the running of the Queen's Plate, wearing a top hat and grey cutaway coat, graciously accepting the traditional purse of golden sovereigns from whichever member of the Royal Family was in attendance that year. Taylor had bred Northern Dancer, Canada's most successful thoroughbred, and had expensive stables both here and in Kentucky.

Charles, as everybody knew, had no interest in any of the family businesses except the horse-breeding, for which he had always had an affinity. He was only a year old (in 1936) when his father began buying horses. His childhood days were often made magical by the special world of the track. At one of the long list of private schools he attended, it was the custom for mail to be distributed during the evening meal. The other boarders received letters from home and juvenile publications. Charles got the *Daily Racing Form*. He also ran the intramural bookmaking operation. All this despite the fact that it was years before he actually saw his first race. When he was eighteen, he stole into the grandstand at Stamford in Niagara Falls (one had to be twenty-one to enter legally). He was aided in this misdemeanour by several track characters. Decades later he was still cultivating their acquaintance, and they his. So bold a pattern did racing mythology make in his life that sometimes, in conversation, he would refer to various important events in his past by first calling to mind the Windfields Farms horse that was triumphant at that time. He would always recall, for instance, that he was assigned to Beijing in 1964, because that was the year of Northern Dancer. Similarly, he recalled that the first meeting with the woman who became his first wife took place in 1970, the year of Nijinsky. The system was contagious. I knew that 1977, the year he achieved literary respectability with his book *Six Journeys*, was the year that a Windfields-bred horse won both the Epsom and the Irish derbies, was named the top horse in Europe and was put to stud for a total of $9 million. It was the year of The Minstrel. When in China, Charles upset the authorities by receiving a telegram that read NORTHERN DANCER FIRST STOP THE SCOUNDREL SECOND STOP HILL RISE THIRD LOVE DAD. The wire referred to the results of the Preakness. Kang Sheng's secret service, the dreaded *Tewu*, naturally thought him a spy.

Charles had embarked on writing and journalism while still quite young (finding in himself the same literary turn of mind as his sister, Judy Mappin, who started a wonderful Montreal bookshop, a mecca for anglophone writers, named The Double Hook, after Sheila Watson's novel). He published a book about his experiences during the early period of the Cultural Revolution, and had run the bureau in Hongkong and initiated the paper's African coverage from an office he set up in Nairobi. He was the consummate pro. He spoke no other language than English but got by on his talent, his charm, his keen eye and his clear disposition. He seemed to have known everyone worthy of knowing—had interviewed Mao, for example—but for the life of him couldn't recall whether he had ever met the Queen. This lapse was not some affectation but rather proof of his lack of pomposity. He was the only person I've ever met who knew the illustrious and notorious Morris Abraham (Two-Gun) Cohen, the *other* famous Canadian adventurer in China between the wars, the one who played the same role *vis-à-vis* Norman Bethune that the Antichrist did to Christ. When Charles knew him, Cohen was some sort of Kuomintang spy in Beijing, claiming, for purposes of a cover-story, to be an aircraft engine salesman for Rolls-Royce. I once asked Charles whether he was acquainted with Han Suyin, the author of a long series of books on China covering fifty years (as well as, coincidentally, *Love Is a Many-Splendoured Thing*). Charles replied yes of course, but he preferred to call her by her baptismal name, Emily.

Although born in Canada, Charles had been conceived, as he liked to boast, at the Dorchester in London, to which he would tip his hat whenever passing along Park Lane. He had gone to England originally to start his journalistic career in a place more outside his father's orbit. Like me in a sense, he found journalism a means of making a living but not of satisfying his desire to write. He once gave me a copy of a play he'd written during this period. It concerned John Brown, the American abolitionist and martyr, whose hanging in 1859 helped to precipitate the U.S. Civil War. For some reason, Charles had written the play in the manner of Brecht. No one wanted to produce it. So Charles, on one of only two occasions when I knew him to use his wealth as a lever, hired a West End theatre, engaged actors and proceeded to mount a production himself. If I recall the story correctly, opening night coincided with a freak blizzard and simultaneous labour disturbances that had shut down both public transport and the Fleet Street presses. Charles had to paper the house, sending runners with fists full of free tickets to hospitals all over central London to lure gangs of off-duty nurses out into the snow. Also, the theatrical costumers in Shaftesbury Avenue had let him down. Shortly before the doors were set to open, his girlfriend was working furiously at a sewing machine set up at centre-stage. Clearly she wasn't going to be able to clothe everyone before the bell at eight o'clock. With seconds to go before the curtain went up, she ordered Charles to take off his trousers and give them to the second male lead.

"The play received one review," Charles remembered sadly. "It was in a magazine that suspended publication the following week." He liked to see these two facts as coincidental.

In all, Charles had worked in more than fifty countries covering stories, including the Six-Day, Biafran
and Vietnam wars. During the first of these, External
Affairs in Ottawa phoned Dic Doyle at the *Globe* to
inform him that Charles had been reported as missing
in action. After agonizing for a while about the fate of
one of his people, Doyle finally had to face the
prospect of passing along the news to old E.P. down in
Nassau. Infuriatingly, no one at the news desk or the
*Globe*'s Report on Business could discover the mil-
lionaire's unlisted telephone number. This scene
played out in Marx Brothers fashion until the number
was located, in full view, on the bulletin board used by
the paper's racing handicapper. Fortunately, Charles
was not hurt or in much danger. He had simply been
lost for a couple of days, the result of a transportation
mix-up, and had been wandering in the desert.

"That sounds uncharacteristically biblical of you,"
I said when he told the story.

We were drinking brandy in a room filled with his
collection of books about China, as he played with his
favourite walking stick, whose handle concealed a
knife blade.

"I was going through a devout phase," he replied.

I got to know him after he had left the paper in
order to write his books but was still contributing
freelance articles. It was, I believe, 1972 when he rang
up to interview me for a piece he was doing about the
poetry-reading scene, and for much of the rest of the
decade we would meet to raise hell and enjoy ourselves. Perhaps he liked my company because he was
such an enthusiastic collector of people.

Charles was an awe-inspiring drinker, preferring Scotch neat. "No ice," he would say, mimicking some old duffer he knew from the Long Bar at Raffles in Singapore. "Damn stuff sank the *Titanic*." He was also a lover of good food. I once had to administer the Heimlich manoeuvre when, presiding at his favourite table at one of his favourite restaurants, he started to choke uncontrollably and his naturally pinkish face turned fire-engine red. Another time I wouldn't let him drive his BMW home but insisted he spend the night in the humble guest bed until he had sobered up. I gave him towels, a toothbrush and an alarm clock. He departed about 6:00 a.m. He was trying to be quiet but there was a certain amount of fumbling along the corridor and challenges from Heywood the dog. From my insomniac's window above I could see him setting off in the snow with only one glove and one galosh, looking like a man trying to remember where or whether he'd parked.

Which is to say that Charles had his demons, like the rest of us. His were simply more public because his father was such a public figure, though the two men couldn't have been more different politically, for example. Charles was a Canadian nationalist in the Red Tory tradition and wrote an important book on Canadian complicity in the American war in Vietnam. But his most fondly recalled book will always be *Six Portraits*. It has pretensions to a political thesis (one he fleshed out more clearly in *Radical Tories*, a study of Al Purdy, George Grant and others) but is in fact a series of biographical sketches of splendidly colourful Canadian eccentrics, well known and otherwise: a book both Sitwellian and Stracheyan in approach but more fun than either would suggest.

He should have produced more books than he did, including a memoir. Lord knows I nagged, cajoled and pleaded with him to funnel his writing energies between covers. He took my advice more to heart than Bob Fulford but was caught up in too many other projects, including a term as chair of the Writers' Union and of course his abiding dedication to self-enjoyment. Too many books vanished as wonderful conversation. I suppose that's one of the prices of having an outgoing personality, which in his case coexisted with the notorious upper-class WASP reticence that is so often diagnosed in Canada's culture but so poorly explained.

One day Charles and I were caught in a sudden rain storm on Bloor Street and I brought out a green-and-white-striped umbrella. He looked at me forlornly. "I'm still trying to get up the courage to get one in brown," he said.

In 1994 I published an experiment in metafiction called *The File on Arthur Moss*, concerning the way conspiracy tends to result from the meeting of technology and politics (I got the idea from the 59th Psalm). The tale was set in the 1970s in Saigon and Toronto and tried to show how the two places were becoming virtually indistinguishable from each other as the toxic spill of American values continued to poison the planet. The title character was the anglophilic East Asian correspondent of a mythical newspaper I called (after groping for a name) the *Globe*. Journalists dumped on the book, as expected, because it tried to raise questions about what journalism is for, but the work generally found favour with the literary audience, as I had hoped. One or two columnists were brazen enough to suggest that the novella was a *roman-à-clef,* with Arthur Moss a thinly disguised Charles Taylor. This was a charge that Charles graciously joined me in denying. The fictional Moss, for one thing, is clearly one of the world's least talented reporters. Charles Taylor was the opposite.

———————

I write this in 1996 when our various levels of government are dismantling the support structure for Canadian culture that has been built up over the decades, with the greatest strides for writing and publishing having come in the noisy and contentious seventies. Those of us who work in the arts all view the present with disgust and the future with dread and the past with—what? Loss? Certainly. Maybe also a *trompe l'oeil* pride in what was in fact achieved. For me, the equation contains some special ingredients. This was my period of frenetic on-the-job apprenticeship, my slow maturity, when I more or less produced a very great deal that was panned, vilified or ignored, a period when, having established myself once, I kept having to stage comebacks after each assault on the integrity of what I was doing. When I look back at this period (actually about seventeen years, from 1968 to 1985, when I got my first favourable review of any consequence), I must always be alert not to confuse people's personal malice with the professional type. Maintaining the distinction enough to see the wounds contextually—to "walk the cat back," as the intelligence community likes to say—has been intellectually difficult at times. Curiously, though, I believe it's made me more humane and just, which is all to the good as the character I must have been in the 1970s was, when I look back on him now, not often a particularly engaging fellow.

I see the faces of the people who controlled the infrastructure of Canadian literature, which they had shamed the government into supporting. With a few exceptions, they were generally suspicious of me and whatever work I had done to assist in the transition. Because I had been born in the U.S. and was an anti-American, I could never be taken on an equal footing with native-born Canadians who thought as I did, and of course I was often met with disgust by others born in the States, all of whom, with exceptions I could tally on my fingers and toes, had been indoctrinated in the American faith, to which they thought I was a traitor. A difficult situation, indeed, as, through the decade, people from America came to occupy more and more of the second- and even top-level positions not just in Canadian universities (a major scandal of the period) but also in Canadian culture generally. Yet I'd rather be a second-rate Canadian than a top-grade American. Or more accurately, I'd rather be a third-class Canadian citizen than a first-class American, since no Canadian born in the U.S. could ever truly be the equal of a person who has come to Canada from some third locality. Such is the unspoken code, a sort of secular version of original sin, which I agreed with and bound myself to, only to see it broken in the following decade when Canadian feminists, somehow deciding that there was no special national character to their feminism (nothing like the Greenham Common ethic in the UK that set British feminists apart), began treating U.S.-born colleagues as their equals and, in many cases, their models. Of course that left unresolved the question of how to treat U.S.-born males. But since we were male, we were already inferior. No one questioned any of this. Certainly not I, for I agreed with it. But I didn't agree out loud, since my opinion was worthless and there was no room for me in the debate. Also, to have spoken up anyway, even though the issue was the most important one around, affecting the whole society, would have been to insert myself unnaturally in the workings of the world, as journalists always seem to be doing. I was trying to get away from journalism, move around it somehow, fly beneath its radar, even while using it for support. People in those days spoke and wrote with tiresome regularity of the New Journalism, generally unaware that the term had been recurring, with different meanings, for more than a century. To them the New Journalism meant interjecting some of their own personalities, even introducing themselves as characters, into an article. I was interested in something quite different: conceptual journalism, as I guess you could call it if a gun were held to your head. I wanted to live a life as a writer that would itself be a critique of journalism, exposing its hopeless limitations as well as positing a few ways around them. Something more like the old nineteenth-century man-of-letters (an occupation so thoroughly obsolete that the term remains gender specific). The writers I admired were the new fictional voices that flooded the scene in the 1970s, overshadowing the Canadian poets who had seemed so remarkably profuse in the sixties—writers like Marian Engel, Timothy Findley, Alice Munro, Jane Rule and Audrey Thomas; these and the writers (there was some overlapping) who were bringing a new regional awareness to the scene, one that seemed a necessary prelude to the strong countervailing multicultural wind soon to begin blowing from the other direction. But the writers on whom I actually thought I was modelling myself were public critics. I was glued to an influential book of this time, *The Rise and Fall of the English Man of Letters*, by John Gross, who would later become editor of the *Times Literary Supplement* (and whom I would once offend inadvertently—I could see it on his face—by referring to the favourite *TLS* pub as his "local"— damn working-class colonial). Gross's book told the tale of Dixon Scott and A. St John (pronounced of course Sinjin) Adcock and, to move a bit further up the scale, Lord Morley or Maurice Hewlett or Sir Edmund Gosse—literary johnnies who were generalists in late Victorian and Edwardian times, writing about culture from the unchallenged assumption that it was a matter of broad public concern to an educated laity. Towards the end of the 1970s one of the currents in the Writers' Union was for removal of consideration of serious biography, criticism and *belles lettres* as a category for recognition and its replacement with "creative non-fiction." In practice, this meant giving public money and awards to journalists for doing in journalistic books what they could no longer easily do in periodicals, now that the Canadian magazine trade was dying. The few remaining belle-lettrists were left to adapt or perish.

This was part of a broader phenomenon in Canadian society at the time that most of us who have lived through it (everyone but the rich) have come to regret in some measure or another: the accelerated Americanization. So in that part of the 1970s when other people were busy adopting middle initials, to look more American, I worked hard to keep close to the centre of things but was always pushed to the outer ring by a kind of centrifugal force. My situation made for some curious emotions and attitudes ("It's fascinating," my future spouse would say one day, "living with a person with only half a past." And she knew only the half of it). But my position also brought certain dangers. It seems to me that I was working round the clock in the cane fields of Canadian culture. I couldn't allow attention to focus on me or I'd be vilified. I had to keep promoting others in order to keep from being written about myself. Of course, the vilification happened anyway, from time to time. I look over my shoulder at the books I have written or edited and see that each one for the first seventeen years was the subject of at least one witheringly painful public attack, attacks in which others took such obvious delight. Hell, people would telephone, sometimes people I didn't even know, to cackle their agreement. In such pieces I would be called a person without talent, a writer *manqué*, a stupid person and an upstart foreigner disrespectful of his betters. A fellow poet, as fellow poets are wont to do, once wrote a long piece calling me a thief, without explaining; I have no idea what *that* was about. I had come of age across the border when a common saying, on placards, bumper-stickers and the like, was AMERICA: LOVE IT OR LEAVE IT. I viewed the slogan as a straightforward choice that admitted no ambiguity whatever. But when people sometimes expressed a wish that I would get out of their Canada, I only dug in all the more deeply. I couldn't help being marginalized—the painful slowness of my socialization as a person was alone enough to guarantee that. But I'd be damned if I would disappear.

The attacks always stung bitterly and made me feel, often for weeks or even a month, that I couldn't go on. Friends like Fulford were probably all sick to death of hearing me lay out my latest plan to break the cycle, which actually, of course, is the cycle of my depression and its related bio-chemical speech problems. "I understand what you must be going through," I can hear Bob's soothing voice say with charity and comfort over lunch. "But just off the top of my head, I can think of the following six reasons why you'd shouldn't accept this offer to manage a rock band. . . ." He rattled them off in order of importance as he cut away at his meal as though his knife were a scalpel and his fork a retractor. He was always right of course, and by the time I recognized this, by the time I realized I could still go on, I had in fact been up and running again for weeks. To outsiders, it must have looked as though nothing at all had happened. I often imagined going to some other city to live, but I never did—didn't dare to, didn't wish to. All of this—my sensitivity and the strength of the vitriol—began to change quickly in the mid-1980s, since which time reaction to my work has improved to about fifty/fifty.

There are a number of reasons for the improvement. One factor, I suppose, was that as I started out young, I had always been thrown in among people much older than myself, so that it took a few years for others my age to coalesce in the public's mind. Another, I gather, was that I seemed such an exotic— "not the right sort of chap at all," as I was told after applying for a job for which I was in fact the one absolutely perfectly qualified chap in the entire world—in all the ways, that is, except the unimportant cosmetic ones. I was incapable of willing a favourable first impression on others—and the essential fact about a first impression, after all, is that one gets only a single shot at it. I look back now, trying to see how I must have appeared to those I was meeting. Peggy Atwood once confided in me—helpfully, she hoped—that So-and-so had no alternative but to hate me because I wore a beard, indeed that he disliked the beard far more than the face under it and the person under the face, so I should either shave or toughen up, one or the other. Sound Atwoodian advice, that. But I knew barbering wasn't the answer. When I think back and see the tall misshapen figure I was, I hear someone who had virtually all the interlocking problems of the stutterer—the repetition or elongation of certain sounds separated by god-awful silences and mismanagement of breath. Worst of all for face-to-face communication was my inability to keep in natural eye-contact with anyone I was speaking to. When I did manage to talk, I would have to look at right angles to the person's face, or, worse, cover my twisted mouth behind my cupped hand (which of course only made me more difficult to hear). All this derives from shame, shame at not being able to talk, the daily situational shame superimposed on the life-long residual shame. One becomes ashamed of being ashamed, and the result is self-loathing.

In a phrase, I was not smooth. I was not, in a word, polished. In recalling those who were glib or slick, I come up against the fact that honesty should have made me recognize that I was jealous of how articulate they were. But self-knowledge is the hardest to come by and has the longest gestation period of any form of intelligence. At the time, I was inclined to moan (only to myself, I hope) that in fact it was *not* the meek who seemed always to inherit the Earth but the slick, and I was pretty sore about it too.

I expressed a desire for every job that came up in the new bureaucracy of Canadian culture, in such bodies as the militantly or stridently nationalistic Independent Publishers' Association (IPA) and the Book and Periodical Development Council (BPDC)—the whole alphabet soup of acronyms that was beginning to cook at that time. The leadership was almost entirely male and, in retrospect, often vain or silly and of insufficient stamina. I was always turned down or passed over—finally, with a derisive laugh and a disbelieving shake of the head by one of the leading nationalist theoreticians of the day. Nor did it seem possible for me to be, in any significant way, a beneficiary of the system. I received one small Canada Council writing grant ($3,500) in 1970, none thereafter up to the present time (when the continued existence of the Council is in question). My only real ambition was (and is) to be part of Canadian writing. Yet in the seventies I was a sort of outcast inside Can lit, which was polarized, just as it had been so often in the past, between the nationalist camp on the one hand and the internationalist or cosmopolitan on the other. I felt myself part of the former, of course, but was usually accepted only when my physical presence could be useful to somebody. For example, I was an enthusiastic member of the Writers' Union but never felt comfortable enough to attend meetings or functions. Finally, a bit later in the seventies, when Charles Taylor was set to become chair in a year or two, he persuaded me (and the current chair, Tiff Findley) that I should do some committee work. When my name was raised at the annual general meeting, I believe, there must have been a blackballing—Charles was embarrassed by what happened and would never go into details. So I continued to be a dues-paying member, an observer who wanted to be a participant but could not. That was a convenient metaphor for my general situation in the literary world during much of this decade.

Since I was anathema to the condescending academics—that went without saying—and since I had begun to despair of my ability to find and hold a job, I had to have a plan for survival. My plan was simply to support my unrelenting schedule of personal writing by setting up in private practice as a writer for commercial magazines. I would become a sort of public commentator, giving the public no hint, if I could help it, of the anguish and turmoil I was feeling. Here again, I believe that I was fooling myself alone. Anyone who was likely to see through the shambles of the personality I presented to the world—Charles, for example, or Bob—was both sufficiently sensitive and insufficiently squeamish to recognize what was taking place. I felt at times as if I hadn't taken the road away from professional gambling after all. Only by luck, not by anything I consciously did, or by any force I could control, might I meet people with the patience and plain goodness of heart to overlook what they saw on the surface and try to communicate with me. I liked my friends and worked hard at friendship. It was frustrating, however, not having any real influence on who my friends and colleagues were to be. But I was grateful for every one of them who made it plain, by action, gesture or even psychic transmission, that they sensed in me more than the very little that met their eyes. It's mainly these rare birds whom I chronicle here.

———————

The communal house on Howland had the one great disadvantage of communal houses: what with all the comings and goings, it was almost impossible to do any work requiring concentration. At this point I happened to hear from my old friend Vera Frenkel, the print-maker turned installation artist, that she had a space to rent in a former factory up the street, north of the CPR tracks, on a short stretch of Davenport that always reminds me of Côte des Neiges Road in Montreal, what with the way the small apartment blocks on the opposite side are set into notches in the escarpment and reached by long flights of precipitous concrete steps. Vera and her Israeli husband, Oded, and a few other people had purchased the place. She gave me this information during one of the breakfasts we had fallen to having together each Saturday morning at a greasy spoon on Bloor Street. Vera, who seems to me to represent the mixed-media artists' coming of age as surely as General Idea or some of the people connected to A Space and the other alternative galleries, was then living and working round the corner in a massive and wonderfully inert Annex house, owned by a local rounder and reputed hoodlum who ran the Victory Burlesk on Spadina, a house that looked like an immense old sailing ship that had gone aground. With her delightful throaty laugh, all-powerful intelligence and preference for chaos all around her, Vera would arrive at the restaurant with a short retinue of retainers and student volunteers and a rather large old-fashioned typewriter. While she held court, and the others laughed and ate, Vera would bang away at the keyboard, attending to letters that were sometimes months or even years overdue. Strangely, the other patrons, trying to pry open their eyes with coffee so as to read the Saturday papers in peace, didn't seem to mind Vera's racket. Neither did the owners of the restaurant. Perhaps everybody understood that they were in the presence of a strong female creator, an archetype in the same general classification as Emma Goldman or Isadora Duncan.

Vera had been born in Czechoslovakia, but her family managed to escape to Britain while the Second World War ravaged their community and dehumanized, or worse, their fellow Jews. Vera's voice had no trace of another country, but her penmanship was unmistakably English. I had met her originally one summer day in 1968 on Markham Street, where she and a number of other artists rented studios from David Mirvish above the shops and eating-places that Mirvish and his father, the discount tycoon Honest Ed, would persuade the city to call Mirvish Village. She was sitting at an outdoor café with Bob Davis, the editor of *This Magazine Is About Schools*. She was an energetic and highly disciplined yet comically disorganized woman of about thirty whose large inviting face instantly drew people into her web of art and mischief. That and her unmistakable (it might almost have been copyrighted) laugh.

Vera's father had been a furrier in Montreal, her mother a corset-maker, and she had studied art privately before going to McGill in the 1950s, where she was part of the circle that included Lionel Tiger, the anthropologist, and Leonard Cohen, the neo-Elizabethan who later invented the musical sub-genre I call chamber punk. She had illustrated some of the titles in the famous McGill Poetry Chap Book series, and was herself a poet, subordinately. At one point in her art training she studied under John Lyman, who himself—in 1905, I believe—had studied under Matisse. In later years, Vera told me, Lyman actually grew to resemble the elderly Matisse, with his small white head coming to a point at the bottom in a faint goatee. He also became a bit dotty perhaps.

"In his last period, he and Mrs Lyman would stroll along Sherbrooke Street every morning on their way to have lunch at the Ritz," Vera recalled. "He walked with a stick by then, and may even have been wearing spats. In any case, he sometimes tipped his hat or gave a little wave, acknowledging nonexistent greetings."

Vera's technical understanding was spectacular. She had been taught how to grind her own pigments, for example, and she knew other skills, too, that had come down in a straight line of descent from the Renaissance. She had done an assortment of things for a living, from guiding tourists through the Roman antiquities at the Royal Ontario Museum to (during her Emily Carr phase, perhaps) running a rooming-house. This second establishment, located on Huron Street, catered to artists of all types, including at one point the very young Joni Mitchell, then unknown, who made her money by working in the ladies' coat department at Eaton's, an area she preferred over some other sections of the store, Vera recalled, because she didn't have to wear a hair-net. I suspect that Vera was both a wonderful success and a wretched failure as a landlady—a success in building relationships with all her charges, a failure in not noting when or if they paid their rent. I base this guess partly on her personality—that of a person with a big and intelligent heart, energizing everyone she encounters but sucking all the oxygen out of the room sometimes. I also base it on first-hand experience, for she let me have the spare single room in her studio at some absurdly low rent if I would sweep the stairs and perform other light housekeeping duties whenever I thought of them.

There were two other little studios on either side of mine. One was occupied by an older woman who painted there irregularly: a meticulous person, she was slowly filling the place with immaculately stretched canvases covered in plastic. She was thus the absolute opposite of Vera, who let everything pile up. (In my observation, visual artists stand at either the one extreme or the other, never just slightly neat or only somewhat messy.) The studio on the other side was occupied by a young woman who, to her feigned chagrin and stylized indifference, was the very image of a porno film actress of the day. She lived with a well-known composer and for money she undertook portraits of people's pets. She was the first person I ever met with a serious interest in tattooing and related body decoration for artistic purposes, divorced from anthropology and what's now called body-lore. She didn't stay long, however, and Vera soon reclaimed her old room as additional storage space for electronic equipment.

For this was the period—an important juncture in Canadian art history, I believe—when Vera seemed to be finally and definitely putting works-on-paper behind her and becoming Canada's premier video artist, with her marvellously written responses to the traditional problems of narrative. Her pieces often had a piano score she had composed herself, and they frequently used a cast of her fellow artists, friends and hangers-on. I appeared in one of the installations, *Signs of a Plot: A Text, True Story & Work of Art*, as a cynical journalist. The role was a two-way stretch; I believe she chose me because I already owned the most important prop, a nicely battered fedora (which Charles Taylor, a hat snob, noted with rising eyebrows came from Herbert Johnson's in St James's. "He must be coming up in the world," I thought I heard him say to himself).

Everyone with direct knowledge tells me what a wonderful teacher Vera was, and I could certainly believe them. As the years went by I was frustrated on her behalf that she wasn't better treated in Canada despite being the country's best-known video artist abroad. She had been artist-in-residence at both the Art Institute in Chicago and the Slade School in London, but her mother institution, York University, was fighting with her constantly and her life was forever being made miserable by some philistine at one of the newspapers. Later, when she received the Molson Prize from the Canada Council, those who knew the score were especially pleased.

I was never formally her student and yet, as I believe we both understood, our friendship was very much that of wise teacher and eager pupil. During this period I would see her at least several times each week. She would come staggering up the stairs carrying papers and equipment and found objects (she once got eleven claw-footed bathtubs out of an apartment building that was being razed—eleven, a banker's dozen). Her arrival would likely be attended by a cloud of dust, indicating that I had neglected to sweep. We would go into her studio, a lovely long room with a wall of north-facing windows and all the touches of home. The decor was Landed Bohemia. She had all her books there and an old upright piano and a sort of overstuffed Roman-style sofa that suggested Vienna in the days of histrionic swoons and historically important seductions. And when the two of us were settled in, we would talk and talk and talk, sometimes continuing afterwards at one of the restaurants Vera knew where the food was reasonable and the highly emotional proprietors, imbued with a profound respect for artistes back in the Old Country (wherever that happened to be), would be flattered by her patronage. Their cousins would be summoned from the kitchen to revere the sight of such a customer, but at a polite distance, from behind the latticed partition and the potted palms.

Vera made me understand colour theory and so much else. In general, she taught me how to look. Most of all I learned to accept art as a process not an accumulation of acts, deeds, objects or intentions. Using her memory, and her current classroom methods, she even let me in on many secrets of technique. When people at universities found that my writing was worthless because I have no degree, I would respond with long hydraulic arguments. When the visual artists (a much snobbier bunch than literary academics, in my experience) complain that my work is worthless because I have no accredited training, I simply take Vera's name in vain (I've never told her this and am afraid to now). I imply that my years of informal one-on-one at her place, a kind of unlicensed atelier with many of the attributes of a speakeasy, is my art-school equivalency, adding, "I was also the janitor." That will often shut them up.

———————

The elemental seventiesness of the seventies, as a time when counterculture was cross-fading into millennial conservatism and reaction, isn't lost on me, I hope. I remember the afternoon I dodged through the traffic on Bloor to set foot at the bottom of Albany and find that the latest edition of the *Star* (there were five then, spread throughout the day) was in fact an extra: NIXON RESIGNS. I had been following Nixon's slow downfall closely, as I had once seen the old war-criminal up close when he was giving a speech. He wore a tight little two-piece blue suit that exaggerated his bad posture, and at the end of the performance he extended his arms scarecrow-fashion, his trade-mark gesture of insincere determination. What I remember most clearly, however, is that he was wearing pointy shoes, like a gambler. Of the talk itself I recall absolutely nothing.

My most ardent memory of public events in the outside world impinging on Toronto, this sanctuary without peace, dates to 1972. I was browsing in a bookstore, which is what I was usually doing when I wasn't writing into the night. It was mid-afternoon. A radio was on in the shop. The news came over the speaker that J. Edgar Hoover, director of the FBI since 1924, had finally died and gone to Hell. I was a little shocked, I confess, when a great cheer instantly went up from all the other patrons scattered around the bookshop. On reflection, I realize that this was probably the last historical moment when such a reaction was possible. Toronto was at the absolute crest of its public (as opposed to social) anti-Americanism, and for that and other complicated reasons would never be so livable again.

During this whole period, of course, I was barred from entering the States. When Nixon resigned to avoid impeachment, he was given a retroactive pardon by his former vice-president, Gerald Ford. This made Ford, one of those decent, thick-witted American pols of whom Ronald Reagan was the best loved and most malevolent, into something of a leper. So much so that he was defeated by Jimmy Carter—"not simply a governor of Georgia," as I remember Fulford putting it, "a position that carries with it almost unlimited potential for obscurity, but a *former* governor of Georgia." Carter bravely promised to throw out all the charges against exiled Vietnam draft protesters during his first twenty-four hours in office. He kept the promise. I had recently discovered that the U.S. Department of Justice (Washington, D.C., has a Department of Justice in much the same sense that Hull has a Museum of Civilization) was in the habit of sending all its old wanted circulars to the National Archives. The collection, I learned, could be accessed at least as far back as the 1890s. I was in the mental process of figuring out how I could get a copy of the "fugitive bulletin" on myself. I wished to see whether I could find some way to sue the American government for unauthorized commercial use of my name and image. Before I could do so, a quite different document arrived in the mail. It was the presidential order dismissing the charges against me "with prejudice"—meaning that they couldn't be reinstated.

At this time I was juggling writing assignments from six or eight Toronto magazines and needed a short holiday. Thus I grabbed at a travel piece that *Toronto Life* wanted on "Studs Terkel's Chicago." After being officially at large from the Justice Department since the age of eighteen, I now found myself, at twenty-eight, the honoured guest of the Commerce Department or the Department of the Interior— whichever cabinet office is responsible for promoting tourism. The bureaucracy's ignorant left hand put me up gratis at the poshest hotel in Chicago and sent emissaries to ask if the fruit baskets and flowers were satisfactory. Life is capricious, what else can I say? So I began adding American cities to my travels as my journalistic practice expanded in the bull market. Whenever I was there I felt as though I were doing a black-bag job. Like certain rivers in Mexico, I was called by different names according to the states through which I flowed.

I got reacquainted with some places I had known earlier. I hung out in New Orleans, where, as it developed, I was a former schoolmate of the costumer who supplied all the strippers and snake-dancers in the Quarter and where I briefly got to know the grand-niece of a British prime minister who managed a mob-owned health spa in Metairie, or Fat City, just across the line into Jefferson Parish, and so beyond the grasp (I choose the word carefully) of the New

Orleans Police. I was in Miami the day Meyer Lansky died there and marvelled at the hush that fell over the city. I got into the habit of going to New York to spend time with my friend Nancy Naglin, who had moved there from Toronto and Montreal (where she'd gone to McGill) in order to freelance while trying to write fiction.

We had met while I was at the *Star*. She came in to discuss reviewing books. She was small, with black curly hair and a working-class Boston accent that turned *order*, for example, into *otta*. Like Nat Hentoff or Theodore H. White before her, she was a graduate of the Boston Latin School. Our friendship was cemented that first day. My office at the newspaper was only about eight feet square and crammed with unwanted books on all four sides. Being long-legged, I had put my feet up on the typewriter wing to get comfortable. In doing so, however, I knocked over the ashtray, sending my lighted cigarette rolling behind the file cabinet. Then, in trying to retrieve it, I tipped over the huge glue-pot that was then still a feature of newspaper work. The highly inflammable mucilage was rapidly spreading out across the carpet towards the files, where it would be ignited by the cigarette unless I got there first. Nancy immediately joined me in the crawl space under the desk, trying to get the cigarette out of the way using a coat hanger. Just then the managing editor opened the door to chastise me about something. He saw these two bums, one male, one female, side by each under the desk. He quickly excused himself and shut the door, mumbling something about how he would speak to me later. Nancy and I would always end up in such situations. We became great friends.

She lived in an apartment on Vaughan Road that she kept dark, possibly to disguise the fact that she couldn't afford any furniture. I was able to help her get some work not only at the *Star* but also at *Saturday Night* and other places, and I find that she often appears in my journal from those years as

> cool, level headed, big hearted. She says to me at dinner: "Things might have been better for me if I'd been Jewish in New York, which is a lot different from being Jewish in Boston, or if I didn't talk in this weird way. But what can you do?" I admire her absolute togetherness about herself as a Jew and a woman. Also very funny. "You'd have to be crazy to *convert* to lesbianism," she says. "It's like becoming a Roman Catholic. Who could go out with anyone who really took it seriously?" And talking about a hack job she's doing for a book publisher: "It's the kind of a house where the editors are intimidated by waiters."

Now, in New York as earlier in Toronto, she was, like most freelancers, living a life of complex poverty, with a web of interconnected little projects and sources. She wrote for *Rolling Stone* and others, but her steadiest market was a lesser *Stone* competitor called *Crawdaddy,* edited from 1970 through 1979, when it expired, by Peter Knobler and Greg Mitchell, the latter himself a former *Stone* staffer. They had an office on the west side of Fifth Avenue around 14th

Street, not too far from Nancy's primitive apartment on West 11th past Hudson, where she fashioned profiles of various rockers. The magazine was much more puerile and self-indulgent than most of the others, but editorially it had some nice moments. William S. Burroughs conducted an interview in each issue with someone anomalous, while Abbie Hoffman, the former yippie leader who had had plastic surgery and was living underground, served (who better than someone on the lam?) as travel editor. *Crawdaddy* once sent an investigator to see if he could duplicate the incident at Chappaquiddick, in which Senator Ted Kennedy ruined his chances of the White House by driving drunkenly off a bridge with a female campaign assistant in the car; she drowned while Kennedy was able to get free—and take his time going to the police. The reporter succeeded only in very nearly drowning himself. In the journalistic thinking of the time, this didn't mean that the story proved nothing or was unsound. Quite the contrary. The stunt was the story. As I write this, Knobler and Mitchell have appeared out of dim memory with a *Crawdaddy* anthology called—the perfect title—*Very Seventies*.

With Nancy, who loved anything oddball and dangerous, there were some bizarre times to be had. In New York in those days was an institution called Plato's Retreat, in the cellar of the stately old Ansonia Hotel at 79th Street. Plato's was New York's most famous orgy palace. Couples or single women (no unaccompanied men allowed) paid a flat fee at the door and checked all their clothes in lockers. In the centre was a vast communal Roman bath, with all round it little alcoves and grottos with people engaged in every sort of sex, sometimes in numbers divisible by two and sometimes not. There were also separate orgy rooms, accommodating as many as fifteen on wall-to-wall mattresses, for those who wanted group privacy. The point was to extend the easygoing anonymity of the gay baths to the heterosexual world. The night Nancy and I ended up there it was full of people from Connecticut (they were naked, but you could tell) and the water-soaked carpets went squish-squish underfoot. Nancy and I were old friends but not lovers, and so we agreed to go searching our separate ways and to rendezvous back at the pool at 3:00 a.m. When we met up again, we were both glum-faced. "You mean to say," she asked, her accent becoming thicker with exasperation, "that we're the only two people who can't get laid at an orgy?" We then sized each other up for a moment but both had the same thought at the same instant: *No, I don't think so. But thanks.*

I was always fascinated by stories of her lovers. One was a shrimp-boat captain in the Gulf of Mexico, another a gambler who let people infer, because of his name, that he was a department-store heir. Then she began going out with a fellow who was a staff writer at *Screw*, the New York sex-industry trade paper. He was a shy, likeable chap who wore tight pants with a rat's-tail comb protruding from a back pocket, an overgrown duck's-ass haircut and an open shirt with sleeves rolled up to the shoulder. Through him she too began contributing to *Screw*, using the pseudonym Buddy McCaslin (the name of a minor character in Faulkner's *Go Down, Moses*). They later married, and he became the video critic of the *Daily News*.

Everywhere I went in America I felt a complete stranger, as though I were deceiving the populace there, who were sometimes puzzled by my pronunciation and carriage but were too insular to suppose that a person they would meet might not be one of them somehow. The sensation was curious, more a case of being a spy in someone else's place of origin than of being a tourist in my own past. In any case, I saw nothing that made me revise my views about Americanism at home or abroad. On occasion, I had some fun. In later years—I think it was during one of the research trips connected to my own investigation of the first Kennedy assassination—I was in Washington, staying at the Willard (in whose lobby the term *lobbyist* was coined). I couldn't help but walk along Pennsylvania Avenue to Ninth Street to the J. Edgar Hoover Building, the headquarters of the FBI. With its rough cast concrete exterior and windows like square portholes—suggesting overall a 1950s swimming pool turned inside out and stretched as high as possible—this is surely one of the most hideous examples of late-modernist architecture in all America, a building so ugly that to have named it after Edgar, even in jest, was an insult to transvestites everywhere, living and dead. I spent a pleasant hour outside the main entrance, photographing everyone who entered or left. Let's see how *they* like it, I said to myself.

But mostly America gave me a new world of second-hand, out-of-print and antiquarian bookstores to plunder. I already knew all the Canadian ones almost by heart, and this new freedom to browse in a bigger book market was tantamount to moving up to a post-graduate research library. This was the level at which the States appealed to me by now, as a place to expand my collecting, which was not necessarily of the kind born of connoisseurship—not usually anyway, because I was financially challenged most of the time. I collected, rather, for pedagogic reasons. I built up shelf after shelf of books needed in order to write other books and thus, in performing the labour, learn the subject. I might have two or three large extensive collections—and hence, incipient book manuscripts—going on at any one time. Eventually I would have to sell the collections in order to help finance my next project. I sometimes made more money from the books I collected than from those I wrote.

I offer an example. In the early 1970s, a Toronto publisher started a series of books about cinema. It was short-lived, but produced at least one important and now difficult-to-locate book, *All the Bright Young Men and Women*, a history of the Czech cinema by Josef Skvorecky, the expatriate from Prague and victim of the communist crackdown of 1968. His books, except for his first novel *The Cowards*, which Barney Rosset's innovative and Europhile Grove Press had published in English a few years earlier, were not yet widely known here. I knew him through his friend Joe Medjuck, who was co-owner of *Take One*, a wonderfully eccentric international cinema magazine published from Toronto, where I wrote a column (inevitably). I remember Joe once screening a new print of Leni Riefenstahl's *Triumph of the Will*, a copy whose German soundtrack was subtitled in French. Josef sat in the middle of the darkened room and translated both the German and the French into English for the benefit of some, while simultaneously rendering one or the other into Czech for the benefit of his compatriots in the crowd.

Medjuck (later an executive producer of generally not very interesting but hugely successful Hollywood films) was also the editor of the cinema book series, acquiring manuscripts on behalf of the publisher. Hearing me talk once of Ben Hecht, the late novelist, screenwriter, Zionist and sometime director, he asked me to write a book on him. Of course I never would have attempted an American subject unless a Canadian publisher had suggested it to me. Another problem in this case was that the part of Hecht of most interest to me was his period in Chicago in the late teens and early twenties when he made German expressionist writing (and visual art too) fashionable in America. His long Hollywood career, which was proving fascinating to people as different as Jean-Luc Godard and Pauline Kael, seemed to me his lesser achievement. But I sat down to the business of finding and studying his works.

My observation is that pop culture turns over in complete cycles of approximately forty years, and so starting in the 1960s the books of the 1920s were at their most numerous, and cheapest, in those cathedrals of self-education, the second-hand book stores. I learned about the texture of Hecht's career by collecting the way one would do in preparation for an annotated bibliography: tracing his rise through the little magazines to the slicks and seeing the number of anthology appearances, and the desirability of a blurb over his name, growing year by year, until, finally, as happened so often in that generation of American writers, consorting with Hollywood ruined his literary reputation.

Why didn't I do my research in libraries? Because I had an innate fear of public and university libraries as institutions, a word that triggered a vast set of defences in my anti-authoritarian personality. Gradually, this prejudicial phobia has lessened, under the gentle guidance of such friends as Richard Landon of the Thomas Fisher Rare Book Library at the University of Toronto and David Kotin of the much undervalued Metro Central Reference Library. But in those days I was determined to complete the puzzle one piece at a time. I probably spent three or four years searching for Hechts everywhere I went, until I had a virtually complete collection of first U.S. and British trade editions, limited editions (whose vogue peaked in the 1920s), interesting binding variants and all that sort of thing, including several typescript screenplays and a wad of his holograph letters, not to mention a wall of works in which he was mentioned or discussed. By the time I knew these physical works thoroughly, I knew them critically and historically as well, and the point came when I sat down to begin writing, working late every night in my little office down the hall from Vera's studio.

I required perhaps a year to write the book (I wrote with less facility then, when death seemed more remote). When it was completed, the publisher rejected it on the grounds that it contained big words. I then took it to Malcolm Lester, an independent publisher I admired who had special interests in both cinema and Judaica, both of which headings might be stretched to include *The Five Lives of Ben Hecht*, as the manuscript was now called. Wrenched out of the context of the series for which it had been planned, it was now a rather odd book, but Malcolm duly agreed to publish it after consulting with his business partner, Eve Orpen. Eve was a widely experienced figure around Toronto publishing who had an unusual and somewhat creepy claim to fame: she had once given flowers to Adolf Hitler. In 1938, when she was ten, she had been invited to help make a floral tribute to the Führer during his visit to Vienna, much to the silent horror of Eve's mother, who kept her Jewishness secret. Eve presented the bouquet while on horseback. The crowd was so large and frightening that Eve would suffer seriously from agoraphobia until her last days.

A number of years had now elapsed since the book's inception. It was 1977. Lester & Orpen was, like many houses, just getting into computer typesetting. For that and a parcel of other reasons, the book, to everyone's embarrassment, turned out to have more typographical errors than the 122 that Ben Hecht had claimed as a record for his 1922 work *1001 Afternoons in Chicago*. Far too many for errata to dispose of and, sadly, too many to let Malcolm proceed with a deal he had made to export finished books to the U.S. The *Globe*, pursuing what was then its policy of generating controversy on the book pages, gave the book for review to Jim Christy, who as far as I know had no particular interest in any of Hecht's lives but apparently harboured some resentment against me stemming from his affair with Rachel. He dismissed the book, suggesting it was immoral to write about a terrorist (Hecht had been a key U.S. fundraiser for the Irgun, the group that had blown up the King David Hotel in Jerusalem)——especially a terrorist nobody was interested in. "Who cares?" he wrote. That sealed the fate of the book, which accordingly sold about 125 copies before a merciful remaindering, netting me perhaps a thousand dollars for all my work, much less than I received for my Hecht collection when I disposed of it later to a university in Illinois. Some review copies got out to the States, however, and paradoxically there were positive notices in such disparate publications as *Variety* and *Publishers Weekly*, and also a number from abroad, in several languages, since Hecht was and remains a subject of cult interest here and there. The episode was typical of my book-publishing life during the seventies. In fact, it could almost be said to be only slightly less typical of Toronto publishing in the same period, when everything was slapdash entrepreneurship. The one good result of this particular experience was a slowly evolving friendship with Malcolm Lester, who doggedly and bravely labours on as an independent publisher of quality Canadian books in a hostile political and economic environment.

# CHAPTER THREE

# A Second-Hand Education

**W**ORKING ALONE at nights in my little corner of Vera's enormous studio building I used to get telephone calls from Glenn Gould, the genius of the keyboard who, by a coincidence that I think surprised them both, had grown up next door to Robert Fulford in "the Beach," as such people would insist on calling it, never using the Beaches, plural, the way a younger generation did. I had started to concern myself with the slender question of whether there could be such a thing as a distinct Canadian sound in popular music, and was just beginning, in *Saturday Night* and other places, the linked essays on this subject that much later became a book called *Some Day Soon*. Once I attracted Gould's eccentric notice by something I had published, he was quite sympathetic, though not very helpful. He had once tried to listen critically to some rock songs, and to write about them analytically, but he found the stuff so simple-minded in structure and sentimental in intent as to be impossible, he told me one night. He did, however, write a loving essay on Petula Clark's song "Downtown."

Gould was a nocturnal creature who preferred communicating by phone. At any one moment he seemed to have a regular list of favourite listeners (it would be an error to say that we were interlocutors), whom he would ring in rotation, droning on for hours. One imagined him at the end of the line, sitting alone at home, still wearing the gloves, muffler, overcoat and cap that were the trademarks of his non-conformity.

There were still many such interesting intellectual characters around Toronto in those days. Walking between the house and Vera's I would often see Jane Jacobs, author of *The Death and Life of Great American Cities*. This slow-moving, somewhat mole-like woman, the most important mind in urban planning, lived only a short distance away in a big old Annex house with a vegetable garden on the roof. In the subway I would often encounter Northrop Frye, sitting alone, looking, as I noted in my journal, "like a flasher too timid to act."

I am reminded that Frye, writing about the future of the book in one of the essays in *Spiritus Mundi*, falls to reminiscing uncharacteristically about his university days during the Depression. He recalls that Toronto then "still had a good deal of the British midland town about it, including a number of second-hand bookshops," where one was drawn inexorably into a different emotional and intellectual relationship with books from the kind experienced by the student on campus. Frye's contemporary Robertson

Davies spoke affectionately of the same Toronto book dealers in a short talk he gave at the opening of the 21st Annual Toronto Antiquarian Book Fair in 1993 (it was published as a booklet, one might almost say as a bibelot). For if it's only in the decade I am writing about that Toronto's antiquarian book community became a significant dot on the international map, the city's roots in the business go fairly deep. William Johnson, a full-time bookseller (not the druggist-bookseller or the stationer-bookseller of colonial times), was issuing catalogues of out-of-print books from 312 Yonge Street well over a century ago, for example. Yet it is only the names from the 1930s and 1940s, the ones Frye and Davies were thinking of, that still set off a faint bell of recognition in the subconscious of Toronto book lovers.

Inside the front board of many old books you will see the little green label of Tyrrell's Book Shop, which was located on the west side of Yonge, and had an extensive used and antiquarian department. In those days, Canadian bookselling adhered more closely to the old British practice, with new and second-hand books under one roof. Eaton's once had a second-hand book department, for instance. At one time, Tyrrell's used-book section was operated by Harold Creasser, who left to start his own shop a few doors away, on the southwest corner of Yonge and Yorkville, specializing in Canadiana. This was a brave subject to cultivate in those days, when only the formidably well-connected Dora Hood and her successors, with her Royal warrant from Buckingham Palace as purveyors of Canadiana to Her Majesty the Queen, were paying much attention to it. "He was a nice man with a great love of books," Blair Laing wrote of Creasser in *Memoirs of an Art Dealer*, "and his prices were so low [that good books] cost almost nothing in his shop; just a few interested characters kept him going." The first part of the description, like the last, could be applied to so many later dealers as well, including those I am remembering here.

Also to be found along Yonge Street was the Albert Britnell Book Shop, an institution that has persisted in the same location since 1892, though it long since abandoned both of the distinctions for which it was most interesting. The first was the reputation for being the toniest of bookstores outside Hatchards in Piccadilly, staffed (overstaffed, in fact) by pearl-laden ladies who knew nothing much about books but spoke in English accents that had long since vanished from Britain itself, in much the same way that some traits of Elizabethan speech are said to linger in the remotest parts of Appalachia and the Ozarks. The second claim to fame was Britnell's second-hand department.

In his talk to the antiquarian book fair, Davies mentioned that his father, Senator Rupert Davies, had been a customer of the original Albert Britnell who had in fact been in the second-hand book trade from 1885, years before opening the shop. One gets a glimpse of Albert in a privately printed 1923 booklet, *Books and Booksellers in Ancient and Modern Times: With Autobiographical Experiences of the Past Sixty Years*, by his younger brother John Britnell, a work that notwithstanding its title seems mainly to be about Christianity. Anyway, when most people alive and reading today think of Britnell's they refer to the shop under the management of the founder's son Roy, who kept up the antiquarian department until his death in 1983.

Roy Britnell was probably the last man in Toronto to wear spats. Certainly he was the last to wear them as a matter of routine, without affectation. He liked to taunt the full-time antiquarian dealers with hints of all the treasures that came his way from Rosedale mansions. The stories quite often turned out to be true, for he was the antiquarian bookseller to Toronto's carriage trade, until Hugh Anson-Cartwright (who also grew up near Fulford and Glenn Gould) assumed that now sadly obsolescent role. It is a position quite different from that of being a top-end international dealer like the former socialist who started out in the seventies selling political books from an old house near the Bathurst Street subway station and rose to become, in dollar volume and in commanding style, Canada's top dealer of rarities—but whom I can't identify here because he threatens to sue me whenever I mention his name in print. (Antiquarianism tends to make people grumpy by constantly proving the superiority of the past over the present.)

Roy Britnell, whom Robertson Davies recalled as "a raging Liberal," like Senator Davies, got the future novelist interested in books when he was only a young schoolboy with prize money to be spent. Britnell "showed great patience and kindness in helping me to lay out the money to best advantage," Davies would recall. "It seemed to be all kindness, but he may have known that he was acquiring an addict to his special drug who would haunt his shop until the day he died." Britnell, who had relinquished the rest of the business to his son Barry but jealously guarded the out-of-print portion, was still very much like that when I started to patronize him.

The out-of-print book world is a ridiculous place to some, a mysterious one to others. The variety of dealers, which started to grow far wider in the 1970s and has continued in this direction, is homogeneous compared with the variety of collectors, no two of whom are alike in their interests. Of course, some people go into second-hand bookstores only to get slightly used copies of current titles at half the new price. As far as it goes that's a perfectly legitimate use of the system, though it's a bit like joining a strict religious order to cut down on one's food bill. At the other extreme are those who collect books as art objects, taking sensual pleasure in the aesthetic interaction of well-executed typography, old paper and fine binding. But in between are the vast majority who are collecting what the books contain and do so as an educational experience with perhaps some nodding appreciation of the books' purely tactile qualities.

At any one moment, only the smallest percentage of the world's books are in print and only the smallest imaginable sliver of that fraction can be found in retail stores. The antiquarian book trade thus performs its most important function in keeping the cumulative past alive, providing an instrument for the perpetuation of old literature, old art, old information, old understanding. Some would argue that this is a job for libraries. Up to a point, they're right, though institutions tend to entomb what they acquire and to exclude the generality of people. At best, there is a healthy symbiotic relationship between a library and the collector's world. But one of the marks of this poor cousin of the book trade—and one of its real strengths—is its fierce independence from authority, its belief that knowledge, connoisseurship, even scholarship should not be public-sector monopolies. Collectors are the foot soldiers in the battle to keep the universities from believing that they are the sole distributors of learning.

People become expert in the most obscure as well as the most widely recognized subjects. One of Toronto's most famous book collectors of this period spent more than twenty-five years building up over ten thousand individual publications by and about Bertrand Russell, only to donate the whole collection to the Fisher library—and then start over again. Another is almost equally prodigious with respect to books about magic and conjuring; still other local bibliophiles put together world-famous collections (that is, in the small collecting world) of Dickens and Lewis Carroll. During the period I write about in the Toronto book trade, Stillman Drake was assembling his collection of Galileo, which was the source for his biography and many other works about the scientist.

My own central achievement in the 1970s—it nearly killed me—was to begin assessing my past, with its inherited difficulties and the ones I made for myself, with a view towards remaking my personality. I don't mean simply a lofty version of a New Year's resolution or withdrawal into one of the therapeutic fashions with which the seventies were littered. No mere cosmetic make-over. I mean tearing down the existing personality through abuse, fasting, deprivation, silence and the most intense clinical experiments on myself that I could devise. I had to mortify the personality that had come with my original packaging, let it rot and fall away, find the hard rubber ball at the centre of being, and build outward from there.

I felt sure I had such a centre (I'm using only secular language here). Indeed, I had some expert opinion on the subject. Some time later, a psychiatrist I was seeing told me that, in view of what he'd learned about my upbringing, it seemed remarkable to him that I wasn't living alone in a furnished room in Parkdale, muttering expletives and eating tins of cat food while standing over the sink in my underwear. His remark offended me at first, but I soon understood what he meant: that I was one tough cookie inside to have come up even to the modest level of civilization I occupied rather uneasily. (Soon afterwards, he fired me as a patient, doing nothing for the self-esteem problem for which I had been seeking help. This was a blow to the chest. But, sure enough, I found the racquet ball inside me and went shopping until I found the perfect shrink, who I believe saved me later on.)

In the bizarre atmosphere of my childhood and adolescence, I was in some ways quick to mature but painfully slow to become socialized. A wide sampling of people found me awkward and mordant. They were constantly telling me so. I didn't have the best genetic materials to work with. My father was debonair in a vernacular sort of way, and this was all to the good. He could also save himself sometimes by his self-deprecating humour and his adaptability to different social situations, tricks I too have picked up. But my mother was hopeless in her bequests: incurably neurotic, at times actually psychotic, and so paranoiac that she could always be depended on to see the most innocent comment in the worst imaginable light. I wanted to be somebody else, my true self, my ancestral self, yet divorced as much as possible from a heritage I distrusted.

This digression may seem out of place, but I feel it isn't. For reinventing the person I wanted to be, not as an actor slipping into a role but really *becoming* him permanently, took up every gill of spirit I possessed. It's for this reason, I see now, that though I turned out books with my usual regularity during the 1970s, and was also working hardest at my assault on the profession of journalism, I in fact wrote nothing in my twenties that seems of any consequence now, save perhaps a few poems from that period—and they are disproportionately few—that I salvaged for my *Selected Poems* years later. The 1980s and 1990s, I think, are when I finally blossomed a bit. In the 1970s, by contrast, my only accomplishment was something just as important but more elusive: reconstructive surgery by a self-taught internist. But then I was self-taught at whatever I was. This is where I return to describing the odd little world of out-of-print and antiquarian books. I was Doktor Frankenstein in reverse: trying to make a human out of old monster parts and, not only that, but then trying to give him an education. I don't mean to write of the latter as though it were in itself some Herculean accomplishment, for I was aided by the times I was passing through. Pound's crotchety works of scattered erudition show the cultural disintegration of his day no less than those of Donne do his. Although of course very different from each another, they were ordinary creatures (Pound, in fact, a yokel and buffoon) who were made great in some way as reflections of the prevailing culture, just as I was free to pick and choose my way through the rubble of European humanism. The Pounds were a quite distinct and more common type than an uncombed genius like Coleridge, a reflection more of a disorganized and brilliant mind, proof perhaps of nothing but statistical inevitability.

In any event, whatever it was I was succeeding in doing, it was done largely in second-hand bookshops. Journalists, who gave me the assignments that paid me the money that permitted me to spend at least one full day a week prowling the shelves for synaptic fixes, taught me virtually nothing, though they sent me to every province and many other countries and brought me face to face, for short periods, with the usual cast of criminals, politicians, actors and other celebrities. What self-improvement I achieved was instead intimately connected to the bookshops and booksellers, many now gone, some still with us, all of whom I remember with trust and affection.

As dealers will tell you, the business is intensely local and wildly international. Scarce and desirable out-of-print books swirl around the Earth in invisible patterns, like ocean currents or flight capital seeking a haven of secrecy. One of the reasons book fairs like the one in Toronto are important is that they bring so many dealers into one room for the intramural trading essential to the whole system. Dealers have tended to become more specialized, selling only crime fiction or children's literature, for example, or even limiting themselves to books about dogs or golf or alpinism (these I've found harder to fathom). At the time of which I write, there was a Toronto dealer named Len Kelly, who as a youth had apprenticed, in the old way, in a famous firm of British booksellers that dealt in only two areas—Methodism and cricket; people outside the world of British consciousness found the pairing bizarre, but of course its logic was impeccable. Professional cricketers—from H.G. Wells's father to the most celebrated of all, W.G. Grace (whose wicket was once taken by Arthur Conan Doyle, admittedly when Grace was very old and Doyle very young)—were all self-made men. That was the point of their being. No inherited wealth or established church for them. They were dissenters—Methodists—in that great line that comes down from Daniel Defoe and the other residents of old dissenters' cemetery at Spitalfields.

Anyway, many such specialty dealers now operate by post or appointment from their homes or upper-floor offices. High rents in most downtown areas have driven out the old-fashioned second-hand bookstores, the kind that by their nature need a lot of space for stock that's not very expensive and turns over with glacial slowness. It's axiomatic in the business that only the dealers who buy their buildings end up other than broke. But I've known many cases where the dealers grew comfortable without owning real estate or else bought their building and died in penury anyway. Antiquarian bookselling is a tradition-laden business, full of conventional wisdom, much of it quaintly and quite patently untrue. Some dealers believe, for example, that Freemasons swear an oath to keep the secrets of their laughable fraternity from falling into the wrong hands and are duty-bound to buy up any Masonic works they see in a bookseller's window. Mind you, some people will believe anything if there's a dollar in it or a free trip to Paradise.

Excepting one or two that are grandfathered, there is scarcely such a thing as a general used bookstore in Manhattan any more, for example. Certainly the booksellers' row on Fourth Avenue that I remember from the 1960s did not survive much after my encounters with it. At times, it seems that Toronto (and Montreal and Vancouver) are going the same way, though this perception didn't seem to be borne out during the 1970s, when, at the zenith, there were probably a dozen important booksellers amid the bistros and other bohemian enterprises along Queen Street West. Also in the 1970s, a smaller booksellers' row sprang up along Harbord Street, west of Spadina, in much closer proximity to the University of Toronto campus than bohemia had ever before been permitted. Several dealers have dealt from all these places, thus illustrating the antiquarian's tenacity, which can be either crusty or placid. For many years, whenever the media wanted to single out an antiquarian book dealer, they seemed to settle on Larry Wallrich, an interesting if sometimes irascible man who died far too young a short time ago. Larry ran About Books with his partner, Toni Greenwood (this during a period when more and more women were becoming dealers and collectors). Larry's was the first second-hand bookstore on Queen. Before that, he had operated from his house. Before *that*, he operated the Phoenix Book Shop in Greenwich Village (Larry was an American who had led a colourful life, including a stint in the merchant marine that ended when he jumped ship in South America). The Phoenix was a famous place of its kind, catering to modernist literary folk. Signed photos of authors covered the walls. In time, Larry wearied of New York and dealt books in London, in Ireland and on Majorca (and towards the end of his life had a second shop, in Copenhagen). When in the mid-1970s he came to Toronto from Europe, he pronounced it the best book town he had seen, given not only the public's interest but also the size of the pool of books, a pool into which three streams—Canadian, American and British—emptied. After leaving Queen Street, starting the out-migration just as he had the original rush, Larry moved the shop to Harbord, where he bought a Victorian house that had the ill luck to be next to the one that housed Dr Henry Morgentaler's abortion clinic. Pro-life terrorists destroyed the clinic one night with a bomb, leaving the bookstore to be reinforced precariously.

The antiquarian book world, a parallel universe to both publishing and academia even though bound inextricably to both, is dependent on tribal custom and folkloric practice. Elders are respected. In Toronto,

the main link to the past of Creasser and that generation is Jerry Sherlock of Joseph Patrick Books, who
kept a shop for many years but now deals from home
in the West End. He got into the trade in the 1940s
when he was a reporter for the *Daily Star*. He specialized in Canadiana, with sub-specialties in Roman
Catholic writers like Chesterton and Belloc and in
theology. He is also the perfect illustration of the
informal system of apprenticeship by which knowledge is shared and perpetuated.

In the mid-1960s, when his shop was on Wellington Street, Sherlock hired a young fellow named
David Mason to work with him. In time, Mason, who
later became the city's leading dealer in nineteenth-
century books, accumulated enough knowledge,
money and stock to venture out, rather tentatively, on
his own. He rented the top floor of Marty Ahvenus's
Village Book Store, which since 1961 had been part of
the little bohemian enclave along Gerrard Street,
between Yonge and Elizabeth, and later became the
busiest second-hand bookshop in the city when it followed the migration down to Queen. As part of the
deal, Mason sometimes helped downstairs, behind the
counter. I still have books I bought from him when he
was starting out. Some have his original pencilled
prices—usually $6 in the case of an expensive book.

Within a few years Mason had graduated to a sub-
stantial shop of his own up the street, the first of several ever more comfortable ones he would come to
inhabit, and various other people were learning the
ropes with Avenhus. One was Nelson Ball, the future
Canadian literature specialist and himself a poet who

has come to be appreciated slowly but with readers' deep affection. Next door to Marty for a while was a dealer named Mitch Cadeau, who was involved in a *ménage à trois* with two female booksellers. The whole community later presented a rare and expensive book to the U of T in Mitch's memory after he was killed in an auto accident. By then, another generation of young booksellers had learned the ropes by working for first Marty or David or both. For one brief moment in the early 1970s, there was an all-night pornographic bookstore on lower Yonge Street that was distinguished from all its rivals by the fact that scarce first editions of Bukowski and other far more obscure modern writers were offered for sale in the glass cases along with the usual dildos and marital aids. Nick Drumboulis and Steven Temple, in succeeding years two of the most important and knowledgeable dealers in Canadian literature, were young fellows looking for work and had been hired by the gangster who ran the place, who gave them a free hand to order what they liked as long as the porn rolled right along. If memory serves, this proprietor, so unintentionally enlightened and unknowing a champion of the avant-garde, was later found floating face-down in the water off the Burlington Skyway. He was doubtless the loser in a difference of opinion with some other patron of the arts.

What was I reading all this time? I had two complementary agendas, which weaved in and out, like branches of ivy.

This period in Canadian literature was a time distinguished, it seems to me, by several shifts. A lot of energetic people were being drawn into publishing, which became so professionalized that by the 1990s, whenever I live through one of the editorial or production snafus that are inevitable from time to time, my consternation is now accompanied by a sharp pain of irony, perhaps somewhat like angina: an attack of the seventies. Mid-decade was an especially interesting period when market roles became confused, with commercial presses taking an unprecedented interest in small-press-type literary works while the small presses tried to gain a toehold in the mainstream marketplace: an era that was all too brief, as the combatants soon returned to their neutral corners.

More important, this was a point when Canadian fiction overtook Canadian poetry as the genre most associated with excellence in Canadian writing, and novelists and short-story writers began finding a solid domestic audience and, surprisingly often, acceptance abroad as well. It was a wonderful time to be a compulsive reader. Women had by now become the dominant force in Canadian writing, a fact that invigorated the whole enterprise and even seemed to charge the air particles electrically, though there were many excellent male writers coming along who did not necessarily seem odd exceptions. This time also marked the beginning of a sort of two-tiered system of Canadian writing. Writing in the various parts of Canada grew more and more distinct from one another. For at least a generation, Atlantic Canada and British Columbia had been as far apart creatively as they are geographically, with the latter being the true creative centre of a Canada from which it nonetheless maintained relationships that were more than just ceremonial. But now other areas were rising, so that regional figures had firm regional audiences and bases of support without being considered in any way second-rate. Often quite the opposite, in fact. Every once in a while one of these holders of a regional reputation would somehow, by a process whose workings I still don't comprehend, suddenly catch on nationally and internationally, as though given a field promotion— breveted in some instances, as the change might turn out to be temporary. This was also the period when Canadian writing began to reflect the multicultural reality. It's telling to recall that in 1972, when Margaret Atwood published *Survival*, her instantly famous thematic survey of Canadian literature, she saw the immigrant novel as a relatively minor genre, represented by books such as *A Stranger and Afraid*, a now totally forgotten work about 1956 Hungarian immigrants by Marika Roberts (a charming woman who later in the seventies ran a Hungarian café on Bloor Street—bean soup that was to die for). Had Peggy written *Survival* only a few years later, it would have been a very different book, taking cognizance of all the Canadian literary energy rooted in non-European cultures and the people who seem to be the important authors now, at the time of this writing.

In any event, one part of my existence, the daylight part, was wrapped up in chronicling and trying to make sense of all this. I don't think there was any point in the 1970s when I wasn't doing at least one regular book column for someone, in addition to stints as a film critic here, music reviewer there, fiction editor at a third place, urban affairs columnist somewhere else. I wrote articles explaining what was happening for the larger public; I organized readings, provided blurbs and prefaces and helped people with their manuscripts. I also, as it discomfits me now to see that I wrote once, "assisted poets into print and, sometimes, out of custody." I lived the freelance's sweet nightmare of ill-paid independence and overlapping deadlines. As my wife likes to deadpan, I have built my entire empire on $100 cheques. In Canadian literature I was less than a full player but more than a mere observer. I was the look-out rather than an on-looker. I drove the get-away car. Sometimes I even got to hold the stakes.

But all this while I had emptied my personality through despair and resolve, the way one empties one's mind through yoga and transcendental meditation, and was set to receive the bounty of my systematic scouring of the out-of-print bookstores. I did this for so long and in such an apparently haphazard way (taking up a book on a subject new to me and letting its bibliography guide my reading thereafter for a while) that it's difficult now to reconstruct the process. But I'll try.

Bela Batta had a tiny bookshop on the east side of Yonge Street, the kind that soon disappeared amid the spiralling rents and didn't resurface again until the late 1980s, when a number of new old-book stores decided to battle what is probably the incredibly heavy volume of unpredictable off-the-street trade: "Listen to them—children of the night! What music they make!" as Bela Lugosi said in *Dracula*. The other Bela's inventory was very small and his warehouse, way out on the Kingsway, to which he denied almost everyone admittance, was very large: he sometimes seemed more of a hoarder of books than a seller. Yet I found a little eighteenth-century edition of *The Advancement of Learning* by Francis Bacon (whom Pope thought must have been "the wisest, brightest, meanest" of the Elizabethans). Through this I got interested in both the Elizabethan political under-world (Christopher Marlowe and such) as well as changing ideas of what constituted knowledge and how it was to be acquired and systematized. This meant going back still further, to the old alchemists such as Cornelius Agrippa, a breed I've often believed had some genuine merit, now lost irretrievably by the coup d'état in which science overturned religion: the most important intellectual event of the nineteenth century, which billions of people still refuse to accept in varying degrees, for various reasons.

Don MacLeod, in his old shop at Pender and Homer in Vancouver, who always kept a few true anti-quarian books (published before 1900—usually well before), practically made me a gift of Camden's *Britannia* in folio, one of the translations of this work from Latin, and I began perusing the antiquaries with vigour. How flat-out mistaken most of them have turned out to have been, yet how noble they were in making their inquiries in what we would call an inter-disciplinary and non-institutionalized way. They were the anarchists of learning, as the French *encyclopedi-astes* of a later time were its foolish authoritarians—Diderot and other people supposing that the world's knowledge could be contained (that is, confined) in a work of several volumes, though this was also the impulse behind the original *Encyclopaedia Britannica*. As for me, like all true bibliophiles and people who care about such things, I sought the never-to-be-surpassed 1911 edition of *Britannica*, scoffing at all later ones as bogus shadows.

I thought that by making a study of the history of what we would call bestsellers I would learn much about the cognitive fashions of earlier times as well as the formation of taste. I collected self-help books, including those whose authors seemed qualified only by virtue of their success in other literary forms: everything from Arnold Bennett's *How to Live Twenty-four Hours a Day* to Robert W. Service's only worthwhile book (and the only one that's never been reprinted), *Why Not Grow Young?*, in which he tells of discovering surprisingly contemporary ideas about diet, exercise and stress after injuring his heart when he took up body-building at fifty—a book whose proof is in the pudding, I suppose, as the "Bard of the Yukon" lived long enough to be interviewed on television by Pierre Berton, dying at eighty-six. And of course I went to the original *Self-Help* (1859) by Samuel Smiles, an author who always makes me think of that wisecrack by Sir James Barrie (of all people), "There is nothing quite so impressive as a Scot on the make." I was interested in exploring such texts as Robert Southey's *Remains of Henry Kirke White*, a work whose abiding popularity with a couple of generations is impossible to figure out today. But I started with Foxe's *Book of Martyrs*, a cheap seventeenth-century edition, ragged, disbound and perforated from years of rodent nibbling, which I bought at Bond's Books on Dunsmuir in Vancouver. This masterpiece of Christian piety, with its horrible engravings of heretics being tortured and disembowelled, was so popular that for two hundred years or so it virtually outsold the Bible in Italy, Spain, France and England.

Ah, England. Among the crimes committed by the Nazis was the destruction in the Blitz of the area behind St Paul's, which had been the centre of printing, publishing, writing and learning for five hundred years. It was as though nothing, not even the air, had been permitted to survive. In trying to reinhabit this vanished space I found myself seeking out books that had been printed at the Sign of the Such-and-such in St Paul's Churchyard. In this way, I stumbled into Defoe as my choice for the most vivid and likeable figure of the eighteenth century (rather than Dr Johnson, many people's favourite, who falls a little later in time with a flourish of bombastic trumpets).

To read Defoe (eventually I was given the most desirable edition, the *Complete Works* published at Oxford in the 1840s) was to be hurled back into his own age when both industrialism and late humanism were rising amid the usual political and religious chaos, and the new London, the one that replaced that which Pepys saw destroyed in the Fire, was truly the centre of the world's spider web. Other Protestant writers, from Bunyan to Swift, always put me off somehow. But Defoe I could conceive of as a whole person—unsuccessful schemer, political operative, hack writer of almost unimaginable fecundity, and only then, finally, a novelist: the first non-fiction novelist, seeking, as someone once observed, a third means of utterance that was neither lying nor telling the truth. He was not simply a wonderful guide but someone who bequeathed his personality to us. I daresay that anyone who participated in the life of Toronto during the 1970s would be familiar with many of the components of Defoe's make-up. There was the Defoe hobbled by his own vanities. (He was a hosiery *factor*, dammit, he replied to his critics' smears, not a shopkeeper.) Except that he was at the centre and not the rim, he is a familiar type even now on the fringes of journalism and publishing: the person who, like Balzac, like Mark Twain, deceives himself into impractical business ventures (at various times Defoe owned a brickworks and bought and sold ships' hulls second-hand). In fact, he was obsessed with business (including the hazards of business, such as piracy), and in *The Compleat English Tradesman* demolishes any romantic notion we may have that daily life was simpler in the past by reason of being less bureaucratic. He was a figure of a thousand projects, practical and wild, selfish and guileless, all designed for the enrichment of society or himself, virtually all of them failures. In that, I suppose, I somewhat resembled him in my role as self-educator.

Thoreau, I thought, instead of building his rude cabin at Walden Pond and producing his painfully repetitious book about it, would have been better advised to continue on in his father's craft of pencil-making, which would have taught him the same lessons of domestic economy combined with a much-needed economy with words. I had a thousand rarefied prejudices. For example, I liked everything by the Goncourt brothers *except* their *Diaries*. Similarly, I was convinced that Lafcadio Hearn should be remembered for what he wrote before he went to Japan, not after. I bolstered my argument when I got hold of a copy of the limited-edition of the great Hearn bibliography by P.D. and Ione Perkins. I bought it at the Mansfield Book Mart in Montreal from Heinz Heinemann, who had fled eastward from the Nazis in Europe only to run into the communists in China (where his children, both of them rare-book dealers like himself, were born). Unfortunately, he lived long enough, into the 1970s, that he must have felt as though rising anti-Semitism might force another move. But he wore no trouble on his round face. He was one of those wonderful old European book dealers whose knowledge ran deep. In my experience, he wouldn't part with a book until he had reviewed it for you, even though several other customers might be queued up at the till. I had already learned the lesson that buying good annotated bibliographies was sometimes successful as the poor person's means of experiencing all the books that he or she couldn't afford. In any event, Mr Heinemann, as I always addressed him, took the prospective purchase from my hands and, as he had a way of doing, let drop a little nugget of autobiography. "Ah," he said in his German accent, "I had another copy of this once. Alas, I was forced to leave it behind in Shanghai." End of story.

I had several of these huge ingestive projects going

on at one time, with dealers in different cities staying alert on my behalf. Despite the fact that he stood for everything I despise except rebellion, I developed a sneaking admiration for books about Andrew Jackson, the first American president who wasn't a Freemason (and therefore, significantly, the first one to be the victim of an assassination attempt—both the assailant's pistols misfired and wiry old Jackson, standing in the Capitol rotunda, caned the fellow to the floor). Another who both repelled and attracted me was Whitman. I was repelled by his caterwauling Americanism. Imagine dating his poems according to the number of years elapsed since independence from Britain, as though he were counting the years of the sovereign's reign, and saying that "these states" were the greatest poem of all. What attracted me was his transition from ink-smeared and gravy-stained old newspaper hack to artist of sorts. This spoke to me forcefully. I have a private theory that Whitman, a great theatre-goer, knew of, if he wasn't actually implicated in, the plot to assassinate Lincoln. His rough-trade lover, Peter Doyle, the horse-car driver, was in the audience at Ford's theatre on the fatal night. But Whitman, who was on some terms of familiarity with both the victim and the shooter, was uncharacteristically absent from the city, and his nursing duties, having gone to New York to see *Drum-Taps* through the press. I came to fancy that I could read the subtext of guilty foreknowledge in "O Captain! My Captain!"

Accustomed as I was to reading the U.S. Constitution looking for loopholes, I reached the conviction, made stronger by time, that the heritage of slavery was the overwhelming source of the American woes that have not only ruined their own society but spilled over into almost everyone else's with such a destructive splash. The problem was not simply slavery but the whites' adamant refusal to let African-Americans into the middle class after the Civil War. Among other things, this resulted in the destruction of America's cities, which were indeed the wonder of the world. Americans may insist that their system of government is what others most admire. In fact, their system is unworkable, and only one of the 150 or so countries that have been formed since the end of the eighteenth century (Liberia—hardly a proud success) has chosen the precise same system of president and bicameral congress. The physical cities, the New Yorks and Chicagos—those were what the world admired. For proof you need look no further than the sort of generic skyscraper city imagined by Brecht or the German expressionists.

Through all this I became interested in the slave narratives, a popular literary form in the nineteenth century, and especially those that touched on the Underground Railroad to Canada and on the communities set up here by some of the 50,000 or so former slaves on this side of the border. This is an episode other Canadians have known too little about for too many years; whatever its deficiencies in racial matters later on, this was one of Canada's finest hours. If I were drawing up the curriculum, Canadian schoolchildren would learn the folk song "No More Auction Block for Me" and know it for the Canadian composition that it is. This in turn led me to slave rebellions (the need for which was no means mitigated by the simple abolition of slavery) and thus to the whole question of uprisings against people who possessed by far the more advanced technology. Which led me eventually to China, a subject that has occupied much of my free-time reading in recent years, but not before I passed through a long period of being quite at home in the 1920s, even to the extent that I could, at one point, after considerable practice, programme my dreams to place me back there in time. I gathered up the Haldeman-Julius Little Blue Books, which did so much to bring art and ideas to the masses, but I was drawn to the cultural critics as much as to the social ones—James Gibbons Huneker and his mentor, Percival Pollard, and various less lofty figures such as Harry Hansen, Francis Hackett and, in Britain, those like Frederic Harrison, H.V. Morton, E.V. Lucas or William Gerhardie—all except the last one names not on the ascent at the moment. I suppose these were a stepping-stone to the all-purpose men- and women-of-letters, varying in quality from Robert Payne of Britain, China and finally America to Jack Lindsay from Australia to John Middleton Murry in England. Such people wrote almost as many books as years they lived—books, seemingly, on any subject that caught their fancy, but always with an underlying unity that gave their published lives dignity, purpose and meaning.

On these subjects I can ramble on almost indefinitely. (One should never invite me to a dinner party without seating me near some strong countervailing force. Otherwise, my wife informs me, I grow danger-ously *ennuyeux* and start giving free medical advice and offering to do the hostess's tax return for her.) My intention here is only to show the unpredictable course such people follow, playing connect-the-dots but always with a bigger goal in mind.

CHAPTER FOUR

# Demon Warriors of New Grub Street

HE SEPTEMBER 1974 issue of *Saturday Night*, the one that was never to be published, was succeeded finally by another, dated May 1975, complete with a new design. The miracle that raised the magazine from the dead, like Lazarus in the Bible story, was greeted with awe, relief and a round of back-slapping, for the period in between had been tough. Some of the staff, such as Bob's trusted assistant, editor Anastasia Erland, had been forced to wander off and find other work, while others were furloughed or let go. The little warren of offices behind Abstainers' Insurance was being kept open partly by a small group of volunteers, including myself and some of the others, such as Morris Wolfe, the magazine's media critic, who had joined together in taking out a big petition in the *Globe and Mail*, urging federal help to prevent the closure.

Already I had known Bob Fulford long enough to

have seen him in many stressful situations in his personal and professional lives, as I would see him in plenty of others. His breakup had been difficult, however delightful his remarriage, and worse was to come. In 1976, his former wife died tragically in a spectacular fire that made the newspapers and the television news shows, while in the early 1980s he would endure a bout of Ménière's disease. Even a flattering offer to leave the chaos of *Saturday Night* to become head of the University of Toronto Press must have been wrenching to turn down. But he stuck with the unwritten code. According to the code, one doesn't leave a ship in trouble; according to the code, the real job of editing *Saturday Night* is to keep the magazine alive and pass it on to another editor, who will inherit the mandate.

Through all these heart-gripping episodes Bob had borne up with great strength, working through the difficulties privately, on his own time, while maintaining radio silence so far as the public went. Partly this was his natural WASP reticence, which he possessed to an unhealthy degree that sometimes limited what he could write, but mainly it was strength of character, pure and simple. Bob was dignity personified, was disdainful of anything that hinted at self-pity. Yet the *Saturday Night* anxiety alone would have done in a weaker person. I never found the right moment to tell him how much I admired his courage and backbone, and I hope he won't be embarrassed if he reads these words now.

While *Saturday Night* was sputtering to what appeared certain this time to be its inglorious end, efforts to revive it, hopeless though they seemed, were already under way. Several years back, ownership had been transferred to a new non-profit organization established for this purpose, so that the magazine might entice corporate donors with the promise of tax-deductible receipts. This approach, which had proved only modestly successful while *Saturday Night* continued to appear, was completely unworkable once the magazine ceased hitting the newsstands. All of us—the informal band of people huddled round the problem, of whom I was certainly the most junior in every respect—contributed ideas for possible donors. Despite his writerly concern for such publishing institutions, I was able to extract only a thousand-dollar promise from Charles Taylor, the richest person I knew. This was due to a trait inherited from his father, who had once, decades earlier, lost a pile (perhaps for the only time in his career) on a magazine venture. It saddens me to report that all of the great and noble-sounding large Canadian-owned corporations, from the Hudson's Bay Company on down, figuratively slammed the door in *Saturday Night*'s face. While the obituaries were being prepared, only Imperial Oil, an American-owned company with an honourable record of supporting Canadian culture, came through, giving $100,000 to the Canada Council with the stipulation that it be passed arm's length to the magazine, no strings attached. In these waning days of Canadian nationalism, *Saturday Night* never ceased hearing criticism of itself for accepting this tainted money. The most amazing response to *Saturday Night*'s rumoured death, however, resulted from a direct-mail piece sent out to the ordinary readers, thousands of whom sent in money for subscriptions they might not ever receive: a touching show of confidence. In direct mail, a response of 1 or 2 per cent is considered successful; *Saturday Night*'s mailing had a 10 per cent return rate. The readers were loyal. There just weren't enough of them.

The saviour of *Saturday Night*, though it later became fashionable to downplay if not overlook his achievement, was a young former advertising executive named Ed Cowan, whom Bob had known, casually, for years. He was a lifelong arts entrepreneur. He was said to have been the person, back in university, who had introduced Ian (Tyson) to Sylvia (Fricker), thus creating one of the most enduring acts of the folk-music boom of the early 1960s. He was still involved in the music business. Indeed, it seemed to me that only a matter of hours before the Canadian Radio-television and Telecommunications Commission laid down its guidelines for Canadian content on the public airwaves, thereby creating a Canadian recording industry overnight, Ed and his friends had opened what was then Toronto's hippest and probably most technologically sophisticated recording studio, Thunder Sound. He was considered a rising star behind the scenes in the Liberal Party. He was youthful, slender, dynamic, and lived with his conspicuous wife, the popular red-headed Irish actor Nuala FitzGerald, in one of the nicer houses in the Annex.

Inflation in intervening years has robbed these figures of their improbability, but Ed's plan called for the sale of $400,000 worth of "units" to restart *Saturday*

*Night* on a sound footing and give it a more stylish package that would attract new readers and finally make the advertising community take it seriously. That he succeeded in raising this capital, and in the middle of one of the worst recessions in years, deserves remembering. One of the two most important investors was Dr Murray Frum, dentist by training, financier in fact, and with his wife, the broadcaster Barbara Frum, a collector, on a heroic scale, of African sculpture. Another investor was the holding company representing Norman Webster and some other members of his old Montreal family. Webster was only about thirty-five but looked younger, with a kind of well-scrubbed boyishness. He had held many jobs at the *Globe and Mail* (a paper once owned by his uncle), including that of Beijing correspondent. In 1983 he would succeed Dic Doyle as the *Globe's* editor-in-chief for a time.

Cowan, who put great store in the necessity of appearances, moved the magazine again, this time to 80 Richmond Street West. The building was small and nondescript but the location fell within the area where most magazine publishing was concentrated. Later, he moved it a second time, to 69 Front Street East, kitty-corner from the Flatiron Building and just across Church Street from Key Publishers, the organization that brought out *Toronto Life*, *Quill & Quire* and many other periodicals. Ed had the large suite of offices professionally redecorated to give the suggestion that really important activity was taking place there. Also, the magazine was of course redesigned, emerging with an all-type cover that I never cared for

(I once unwittingly hurt Bob's feelings by saying that it looked like the little sheet of instructions that came folded up inside a tin of aspirin). Bob, whose big new office commanded a view of the whole city to the north, was busily rethinking the editorial side as well. It was, I see now, a period of shaky transition, in which the old *Saturday Night*, the journal of arts and politics that represented one person's sensibility, was finally, reluctantly, laid to rest as impractical, at least as anything other than a "little" magazine. Bob was trying to expand the journal to attract people in business and the professions as well. Different and more sophisticated political writing, much of it by Christina McCall, Charlotte Gray and Sandra Gwyn, was one of the answers. But the magazine was also wild, unpredictable, designed to show topicality and glibness over seriousness and depth, and the audience was guaranteed a few real clunkers each month (yes, yes, including some by me). What the public didn't know was that Cowan, like so many other terrific idea-men and brainstormers, had less patience with the workaday problems of management. These duties he tried to share with others, including Bob, who now, for the first time, was distracted from writing and editing by additional worries about renewal rates, focus groups, demographics, government relations and a dozen other categories of headache that make up the day of the career publisher—something Bob never was, never claimed to be, indeed most emphatically never wished for.

I remember that during this period he often wore a worried look at lunch when he should have been unwinding.

"You know, we have a terrible problem," he said to me on one of these occasions. "We're not pulling in enough middle-managers aged twenty-four to thirty-six."

At first I thought he was kidding. I would have expected that Bob, the old Bob from the poor days living near the Oom-pah-pah Room or cohabiting with Abstainers', would have taken a defiant point of pride in never having *met* any twenty-four-to-thirty-six-year-old middle-managers, whatever the bloody hell they might be. *Saturday Night* had joined the big time, had gone slick, or was trying to. I felt uncomfortable just dropping into the office now, as I'd been doing for a decade. I felt as though I should make an appointment two weeks ahead and then reconfirm it through an executive assistant. But I continued to arrive unannounced, if only to preserve a fragile sense of continuity. When I did, Bob often seemed unusually glad to see me, almost relieved. I'd close the office door behind me and we would talk about books until the outside world intruded, as it inevitably did, with a series of ominous raps on the door by someone bearing a fresh sheaf of problems.

———————

Once upon a time the major daily newspapers put out special pictorial supplements using rotogravure rather than letterpress. These magazines were done on the special coated stock best suited to the rotogravure process, which involved making the impression from type and engravings that were recessed rather than raised. The result was a product with a rich, liquidy, sometimes almost three-dimensional look to the half-tones, suggesting unusual expense and craftsmanship. People my age can remember when the *Globe and Mail* continued to emit a true rotogravure section each Easter, full of Society ladies who interpreted the story of Christ's death and resurrection in terms of really big hats. It was a rite of spring (like the appearance of the first heroin addict of the year). The technology soon died off but the idea of newspaper supplements, erroneously still called rotos in the trade, remained strong in the 1970s. Newspapers in those days were almost entirely black and white, except for some spot colour ads and a small amount of editorial colour, such as the blue flag atop the front page of the *Star*. The rotos had been created generations earlier to provide a place for colour adverts— and a magazine to help justify the higher price (and maintain the bigger circulations) of the Saturday editions. Rotos were like the stained-glass windows in mediaeval churches: designed to awe the serfs who had few other bright colours in their drab lives.

In their heyday, these publications, such as the *Star Weekly* in Toronto, the *Family Herald* in Montreal and the *Free Press Magazine* in Winnipeg, were great money-spinners for their proprietors and a steady meal ticket for untold numbers of writers and illustrators. Significantly, the roto idea began to wither away, not with the arrival of Canadian television in 1954 but rather with the coming of colour to Canadian television, less than a dozen years later. The once-powerful *Star Weekly* finally shut down in 1969, for example. The *Globe Magazine*, in which I was always proud to appear and that trained a whole gallery of people in the special properties of magazine work, followed in 1971. When the *Telegram*, which had no such magazine unique to itself, folded or was allowed to die, the *Globe* found it cheaper to kill its own roto and pick up the *Tely*'s franchise on *Weekend*, one of two syndicated rotos that competed in cities across the country. The other was *The Canadian*.

*Weekend*, at its most typical (or at least until the editorship was taken over by John Macfarlane, about whom more later), was folksier, more downmarket, more old-fashioned than *The Canadian*. Until its last years, it ran the rip-snortin' huntin' and fishin' yarns of Gregory Clark (whom I once had to interview about his long-ago association with Ernest Hemingway and whom I found to be anything but the kindly old wispy-haired gent of his public image). It is significant that *The Canadian*, which was published on Bay Street in the heart of the financial district and had contracts with the Toronto *Star* and the majority of the other big papers, giving it a reach of a couple of million readers, did not have any subscriber papers east of Montreal, which was very much *Weekend* territory. This was not because *Weekend* was published in Montreal but because it represented an older version of what Canada was, forever just one short generation from the farmstead. By contrast, *The Canadian* was urban and up-to-date. In its brightest period, it was edited by Don Obe, a soft-spoken, shy, intensely dedicated proponent of the liberal tradition and quality journalism for the masses. He was a Métis who had grown up on the Six Nations Reserve near Brantford but was never heard to refer to what must have been his hard-scrabble past. He was different from Fulford in that he wasn't a professional intellectual or a member of the arts community. But he exuded a kind of Fulfordian integrity. Writing for *The Canadian* was seldom a serious matter but was always fun and well paid. I wrote on Canadian writers and publishing, pop music, jazz, photography, film, conceptual art, God knows what all, and travelled nationally and internationally in the bargain. I was living in disguise, as a journalist, and generally loving it, at least during the distracted daylight hours.

Corresponding as they did to my own twenties, the 1970s, as I look back on them now, still seem to have had a freshness about them. Perhaps this perception is a trick of youth. I do believe, however, that there were certain types produced by the seventies without which it would be impossible for me personally to reimagine the time. The decade was the ebb tide of Canadian magazine publishing, for example, and hence the age of the magazine editor as a highly visible and flamboyant character on the scene in a way that did not seem to have been the case at all in the brown-suit Maclean Hunter world of the 1950s and 1960s. That is to say, there had always been magazines and so people to edit them. But the notion of the magazine editor as a creative public personality, blown this way and that by myth and mystique, a setter of fashions and trends no less true (nor more false) than those it was his or her business to ferret out for readers—that, I believe, was a 1970s innovation, at least in Toronto. Like so many of Toronto's innovations, however, it was in fact a ripple of something that had taken place with more force in the States a few years earlier.

American magazines of the 1960s and early 1970s had a special pull on Canadian readers and writers. There is no doubt about that. There was no free trade in magazine talent, as there is today. The publications people admired from the U.S. were accessible but also unknowable in some deeper way that proved they belonged to a different culture that took virtually no notice of our own. People admired William Shawn's *New Yorker*, a magazine I found readable only after the editorship passed to Tina Brown many years later. In fact, given the proper lubrication, I was prone to making a complicated argument that the *New Yorker* was far inferior to *Punch*. Being sober, I won't repeat my convoluted reasoning here, but it had to do with the fact that the *New Yorker* was put out for a large mythical band of individuals—wealthy liberal New York anglos with an interest in the arts, the kind of people who existed mostly in the minds of ad executives (hence the magazine's success) and in the vitriolic imaginings of the *New Yorker*'s own cartoonists, who pilloried this same class and contributed to the illusion of its existence. *Punch*, for all its English schoolboy humour and general lack of sophistication, at least catered to a readership that was mirrored realistically in its pages. That is, the *New Yorker* was published for people who wanted to be like the people in the *New Yorker* but couldn't be, because the ranks were more or less fictional, whereas *Punch* was produced by and for absolutely straight-arrow middle-middle-class English readers with a humour impairment, whose truth was mirrored in every feeble page.

The *New Yorker*'s effect on Canadian journalism mainly took the form of languid longings on the part of people in the magazine business, though there were realistic dissenters. "I laugh whenever a Canadian magazine calls any kind of interview or personality piece a Profile," Hugh Garner used to complain. "The word belongs to the *New Yorker*—one of those long, long highly detailed biographical pieces that take months to research and write and check. Nobody in Canada would spend the kind of money needed to do a Profile in the *New Yorker* sense." Garner was right. Mind you, he was also prone to foreseeable tirades about certain words. He would go into a Garnerian tizzy whenever someone used *chesterfield* for sofa, though he didn't seem to object to the men's overcoat of the same name. Another of his triggers was *fire reels*, a phrase the Toronto newspapers still used for *fire engines*, one of those usages, such as *escaper* for *escapee*, that became rarer and rarer as the daily press became more Americanized. Another American magazine of the period closely read and little emulated was *Ramparts*, the muckraking journal from San Francisco. It had started out as a Catholic literary magazine only to become the home of assassination theorists and the giver to the world of Che Guevera's authentic diaries and all manner of other lovely mischief. This improbable transition came under its one-eyed editor, Warren Hinckle, a San Franciscan of such impeccable pedigree that he could point to the fact that his great-grandmother had been a dance-hall girl in a joint on the Barbary Coast. I believe I met him once, at some anti-conference of anti-media to which we were anti-delegates. (Very seventies.) He was a large equine sort of person, with a glossy black mane, standing, I would judge, about twenty hands high.

But *the* magazine of the time to which all the boozers and doers in Toronto looked with special reverence, and parts of whose editorial and visual personality they regularly tried to emulate, was *Esquire*, then still in its remarkable dozen-year New Journalism heyday under editors such as Harold Hayes. Writing in general-interest magazines in those days was still dominated by the notion of the well-made article, as Broadway had so long been obsessed with the well-made play. Articles in *Maclean's* during its most important period in the 1950s and 1960s had been models of such cookie-cutter craftsmanship. It was a skill easily learned by anyone with a good ear and one almost impossible to break loose from.

"Bright young men were advised to cultivate a good, clear, anonymous style, shorn of personal reference or personal history," Fulford would say of the 1950s in the introduction to his "Marshall Delaney" book. "Reading a journalist in Toronto in those days, you couldn't tell whether he came from Calgary or New Delhi, whether he had had one wife or six, whether he was a Marxist or a Seventh Day Adventist." Bob added: "I mastered this technique, and turned it into even more of a fault that it was otherwise."

But by the 1970s he was unlearning it quickly. Although he never came close to being a self-revelatory

much less confessional type of writer, he certainly out-
grew the Maclean Hunter style to the extent of mocking those who had not. His relationship with Pierre
Berton, for example, was always one of edgy cordial-
ity, as I think he once accused Berton of writing books
that read like 1955 magazine articles. What people
were trying to do now was to insert their own personalities into articles, sometimes even making themselves important characters in the story, and to
develop a trademark style, the way Hunter Thompson
or Tom Wolfe had done.

There was actually an unbroken chain of evidence
that linked *Esquire* to the Toronto magazine world. In
the last few years before its demise in 1971, the
*Telegram*, the organ of the rapidly fading industrial
working-class Tory liver-and-onions city that Toronto
was ceasing to be, was the most improbable hodge-
podge of a metropolitan newspaper you could imagine.
Small pockets of excellence and contemporaneousness
were hidden here and there amid the general run of
stubborn mediocrity and indelible old-fashionedness.
It amazes me to remember now that Susan Swan, the
writer whose performance art of the 1970s metamor-
phosed into her 1980s career as one of the country's
most distinctive and daring experimental novelists,
was once a *Telegram* reporter (their tallest, I'm fairly
certain).

Some of the talent at the paper reposed in a section
called Lifestyle (which represented, as far as I can recall, Toronto's first public embrace of that word, soon
to be as much an emblem of the 1970s as bell-bottom
jeans and eight-track audio-cassette technology). Most

of the rest could be found in Showcase, where Don Obe, Tom Hedley and others were managing to bring magazine techniques to the body of the newspaper broadsheet. Word spread. *Esquire* had its eye on two of the Showcase editors, one of whom was Hedley, a smart, slick, slow-spoken young fellow who somehow fostered a faint suggestion of greatness. Undoubtedly he possessed a certain style not then common in the brown-shoed Canadian media landscape.

"They called me the day before the interview and told me to come in with twenty story ideas," Hedley remembered years later when we were sitting at a little ristorante in Malibu, where he had settled after making his fortune as a screenwriter. "I came up with thirty, of which they took eleven. I'd been up all night and fell asleep in Arnold Gingrich's office. They woke me up to say I had the job." Gingrich was the courtly Canadian (from the same small Ontario town that produced Beland Honderich of the *Star*) who had founded *Esquire* during the Depression.

In that instant, Hedley's career was made. Not his New York career but his one in Toronto, where he returned at about the time the *Tely* was dying and went to work for *Maclean's*. Peter C. Newman had just taken over, with a mandate to make this illustrious national institution, creaking externally and fractious within, into something that worked. The reign of Ralph Allen, the famous editor who had been mentor to Christina McCall and so many others of that generation, had ended in 1960. In the intervening ten years, *Maclean's* had had five different editors. Each appointment had been infused with some of the same suspense and apprehension associated with the cardinals' selection of a new pope in Rome, with crowds waiting below in St Peter's Square for the smoke signal from the chimneys of the Vatican. Now Peter C., as people called him, would be the sixth, and he had the authority to bring order and profitability to the place.

I can't specifically remember seeing Hedley and Peter C. side by side, but what a strange impression they would have made that way. Hedley was cool. He dressed cool, he dated cool. His stint at *Esquire* had given him a certain aura, which he wore like a cloak. He was renowned as a champion conceptualizer, a spinner and vetter of ideas, a child of McLuhan whose genre was spontaneous well-written conversation combined with a basic disdain of the medium in which he was working. He edited by means of what the Germans call *Fingerspitzengefühl*, the feeling in one's fingertips. He was totally disorganized, as though to suggest that paperwork and the mundane practicalities of getting out a magazine were beneath him. He and Obe hung out with painters and other artists at the original Pilot Tavern on Yonge Street— in Hedley's case, in preference to word-people. Hedley was spoken of with awe because the visual side of his brain was said to be so highly developed. He was more a designer than an editor in the normal sense, people avowed; a sort of god-like journalistic being who could somehow command text, image and design to come together, in some process more closely related to physics perhaps than to management. For his part, Peter C. was a more believable and altogether more enduring conundrum. People made sport of him because of his shy, sly personality, the trouble he seemed to have overseeing staff, the number and diversity of his marriages, and his prose style, which was certainly unlike anyone else's.[*] These criticisms always seemed to be based in jealousy at his success and achievements. If people had been intellectually honest they would have acknowledged what a remarkable person he was. A Czech, born in Austria, he had come to Canada as an adolescent wartime Jewish refugee who spoke no English. After virtually inventing modern Canadian political commentary with books like *Renegade in Power*, he had risen to become the editor of the country's biggest paper, the *Star*, and now of its most important magazine, *Maclean's*. But the most extraordinary aspect of Peter was that while clearly a liberal (I can scarcely recall him uttering an opinion that wasn't progressive), he was somehow seen by the business community as their spokesperson, their champion, their voice. It's true that he mythologized them in ways they enjoyed

---

[*] Fulford at *Saturday Night* went through a brief period of using footnotes, perhaps in an attempt to make the magazine attractive to academics as well as to middle-managers aged twenty-four to thirty-six. In writing about Newman, he used a footnote to observe that Newman was the only writer who used footnotes (lots of them), not as a device to inhibit the annotative function that might interrupt the flow of narrative, but rather to highlight all the really juicy anecdotes, so as not to distract readers from the boring stuff in the main text. I explain this in a footnote as an example of the postmodern aesthetic.

(footnotes and all) in his series of books under the general title *The Canadian Establishment*. But this made him a towering paradox. He was a unique (and so invaluable) character in the Canadian political drama because he was the only eminent editor, maybe the only prominent person of any type, who had the voice of those on one side of the socio-economic chasm and the ears of those on the other.

General-interest magazines like *Maclean's* were dying all round us, like elms, and the very concept was being widely obituarized. Peter's plan was to reinvent *Maclean's* as a weekly newsmagazine, once federal legislation drove the so-called Canadian edition of *Time* out of business with changes to the laws regarding the tax deductibility of Canadian magazine advertisements—or rather, changes to what legally constituted a "Canadian" magazine for those purposes. For this and other reasons, the reconstruction of *Maclean's* would be slow and orderly. That is to say, an awkward period followed when *Maclean's* was no longer a monthly of features and columns but not yet a weekly organ of news. It was in this period that Hedley prospered. When he saw that gap closing, he moved to *Toronto Life*, the other important magazine shop of the day. *Toronto Life* was also where almost everybody in time would be editor—except the women in whom reposed much of the magazine talent in the city but who all through the 1970s (and indeed and 1980s and 1990s) continued to perform the managing editor's function of cleaning up the messes of the male conceptualizing geniuses and their respective entourages who followed them everywhere, hanging on their every utterance. Most of the people of my generation with a deep understanding of magazines have been individuals such as Anne Collins, Lynn Cunningham, Sarah Murdoch, Val Ross and Joann Webb. I list only five and do so alphabetically. Almost never have proprietors trusted them with an editor's key to the kingdom, except in the case of "lifestyle" magazines (the term had now taken on profoundly negative connotations, suggesting fashion, food and general triviality). If I were a female journalist, I'd be furious. In fact, I grew increasingly furious on their behalf as the problem continued unabated. Book publishing has been much kinder to women than magazine publishing, and accordingly has siphoned off most of the talent, at least to the extent (a lesser extent than people realize) that the two sectors are complementary, not mutually exclusive.

In the 1970s, *Toronto Life* would become probably the highest-quality city magazine in North America, a far cry from the ones (even *New York*, it always seemed to me) that relied mainly on the breadth of listings—"service journalism"—for renown. *Toronto Life* was owned by Michael de Pencier, an entrepreneur with Old Money who would in time own city magazines and city-service magazines across the continent and round the world, and his friend and more or less silent partner, Phil Greey, whose family had once owned a factory in the series of buildings bounded by Church Street, the Esplanade and Front Street. Phil had set about to re-acquire these properties, add adjoining ones, and then renovate the whole maze for modern use. Phil was the landlord not only of *Toronto Life*, *Key to Toronto* and its sister enterprises in which he had a stake, but also of many literary magazines, small presses and arts organizations of the period. With the daily newspapers (the *Sun* had replaced the *Telegram*) scattered widely along a great stretch of the lakefront, Church and Front became the epicentre of the journalist's dismal trade. Even the people who worked elsewhere in the city came down there for lunch at the trendy little places that sprang up in response (one of which erected a plaque in the booth always occupied by Tom Hedley, proclaiming the space his personal territory). The attraction was not necessarily the food these restaurants served (their menus had listings that run together in my memory as "Julienne of kiwi, reclining seductively on a futon of rice"). The attraction, rather, was the gossip.

---

To continue, not only had every eligible person (male) been editor of *Toronto Life*, but two whom I remember held the post more than once. One of the recidivists was Alexander Ross, known as Sandy, a figure who turned out to be important to my life, not as a friend like Bob Fulford, but as a sort of benevolent antagonist. In fact, Sandy was the reverse of Bob. Sandy had built up a sometimes convincing veneer of slickness and polish, but he was secretly still the Vancouver boy frightened of Toronto (it's easier for the native-born to take such matters seriously, even though the stakes are so very much lower for them). Whereas Fulford, so similar in basic outline if not in the *type* or *level* or *genuineness* of his sophistication, liked me in part because he was more polished than I was, Ross was the opposite, thinking that I was on to his game and was mocking him by my very existence or perhaps just serving as an inconvenient reminder of the nature of his acting.

When I think back on Sandy Ross, I see a transitional figure between the warm-blooded left-wing sixties and the cold-blooded right-wing eighties. I see a perfect representative of the seventies in fact, straddling the two extremes. He *looked* like a sixties person, with frayed blue oxford-cloth shirts and what appeared to be National Health eyeglasses from Britain. He was handsome, square-jawed and appeared younger than his years, bearing a strong resemblance to photographs of Jack London. He had long thick hair that fell across his forehead in a big wedge, which he was forever brushing out of his eyes. He talked some version of the sixties talk and walked some version of the sixties walk. But this was a kind of disguise or entrapment. In reality, he was hard-bitten, cynical, money-driven and conservative. He was more than pro-business, in the way that Peter C. appeared to be but wasn't, not really; Ross doted on executives as the natural rulers of society. This of course meant being pro-American as well. He told me once, in idle conversation, that he thought the Americans had every right to run Latin America militarily any way they chose (I guess we must have been talking about Salvador Allende, whom the Chileans elected fairly and democratically but whom Washington then had assassinated because he was too far left for their taste).

"After all," Sandy said, "it's their back yard." I had never met anyone who believed in the Monroe Doctrine of 1823 with such depth and matter-of-factness. Yet he had a kind of animating magic about him. Charisma, I suppose. He had probably been called a genius more often than anyone else in the Canadian media (where the term is used much the same way *artist* is used in show business).

Like Don Obe and so many other undeniably talented people of his generation, he had started out on the Vancouver *Sun* when it was in the green-domed tower, facing the *Province* across Victory Square. I never quite got the story straight, but his move from there to *Maclean's* in Toronto in the 1960s had something to do with a satirical song he'd written about B.C. politics called, if I remember rightly, "God and Social Credit." From there he went on to be a columnist with the *Financial Post* (bringing in, no doubt, thousands of readers who had never picked up the paper before), a daily columnist with the *Star*, and finally the sixth editor of *Toronto Life*, the one under whom it started making a profit at last. Among his other claims to renown was that he had written the so-called Davey Report, the findings of a Senate committee on media concentration. This document was widely hailed as the only government publication anyone could remember that was memorable for being well written (not that it encouraged the government to take any action of course).

I had known Ross casually in most of his jobs, but we were not closely connected. Indeed, I was the slightest bit chary of him because of an incident a few years earlier during a dinner party at a rival editor's house. Sandy's wife at the time sat across from me in a dress composed of layer upon layer of white gauze-like material—on the bodice of which I accidentally spilled a whole glass of red wine, which instantly spread out in a gigantic ineradicable stain in the shape of Madagascar. That took some spirited apologizing. But one day Sandy approached me, full of admiration about the column of media criticism I was doing every month in *Quill & Quire*. Would I write an article in the same vein for *Toronto Life*? After some discussion, I agreed to do a piece about office politics at the *Globe and Mail*. As I got into it, though, the article tuned out to be much more than that: it became, I like to think, a study of what it was then fashionable to call the corporate culture, of how decisions were made in certain ways because of precedents so long in the past that few now living could recollect the exact details that had set the invisible momentum in motion. The piece ended up being 25,000 words or so, longer than any article published in Toronto that people could remember. This helped create a fashion for terribly long articles, such as Val Ross's memorable excoriation of the labour and environmental practices of Inco, the giant mining company. But the fashion came crashing down some years later, when the Reichmann family sued *Toronto Life* over an even longer article by another freelancer. The magazine, whose insurers spent more than a million in lawyers' fees, might have gone belly up if the Reichmanns hadn't decided finally to let the proprietors settle by paying out some giant undisclosed sum and printing an abject apology.

By the time I turned in my piece on the *Globe*, Sandy had left *Toronto Life* for his next magazine, *Canadian Business*, which was about to begin a new existence one floor below, and I dealt with the person who had been named the new editor because he didn't have a chair when the music stopped: Tom Hedley. They both professed to be wild about the piece. (So much so that Sandy, to his credit, suggested to Tom that I should be paid a bonus, which I was.) As I look back on the article now, it doesn't seem a particularly riveting job of work, though I did manage to synthesize much of the *Globe* folklore, which until then had lived mainly in the oral dimension. Also, as a prophet I would turn out to be uproariously inadequate, though I did accurately predict, strongly but between the lines, that the next owner of the *Globe*, whoever that would be, would break up Dic Doyle's so-called Chatham Mafia and scatter them to the winds. Nor was presentation of the article helped by the fact that the cutlines under a number of executives' photographs got mixed up, even though I had gone into the office and carefully written the individuals' last names on the backs of the eight-by-ten glossies. Maybe errors of that magnitude were inevitable when the torch was being passed between two such non-detail personalities as Sandy and Tom, who were known to delegate such trifles to people who wouldn't come asking questions and dragging them back into the gritty details of production.

Despite all its shortcomings, the article became the talk of the town, in a way that I couldn't imagine ever being true of anything else I might write. Certainly it's never happened since that I've walked into a party to find myself in the middle of a scrum, with people shouting questions at me over one another's heads. I've never seen a mere magazine article, in a local magazine at that, stir up a storm of approval so intense and long-lived. I wasn't certain whether I liked my position or not. For one thing, it seemed a long way from literature. But as I could have foreseen, the attention brought trouble later, though overall its effects for me personally were of the first importance.

All this freelancing was a stressful business. Some months I took in an enormous amount of money, but was always broke or nearly so. At other times, I would become conscious of the invisible wires of advertising revenue that linked me to the big abstraction called the economy—would become conscious of them because suddenly the slack would play out and I would be jerked back into months of penury and semi-idleness. Also, some of the practices that I valued seemed only to tick people off. When, as inevitably happens from time to time, a commissioned article has to be rejected because it has gone stale or can't be made to work, industry custom dictates that the writer be paid a kill fee of 50 per cent. I was always uncomfortable about accepting these, just as I was uneasy with the custom of certain editors—a minority really—of buying only your byline, discarding virtually all of what you'd written and substituting whatever they wished. The first circumstance seemed to be poor business on the writer's part. I held, along with the late Timothy Eaton, that if goods weren't satisfactory then the customer should have the purchase price cheerfully refunded. The other practice struck me as, at worst, a type of proscription (outlawed in *Magna Carta*, I'm sure) and, at best, a kind of ghostwriting. The latter is an honourable enough labour when it's employed to help the semi-literate to communicate their message, as the scriveners do who are to be found in certain public squares in India or Mexico, but not when it's a ploy in some magazine editor's elaborate game. So it was that I got a bad reputation in some circles either for refusing to accept payment for work I'd done that wasn't in the end satisfactory (returning a kill fee made the accountants' lives terrible, it seemed) or else for protesting the use of my name on something I hadn't actually written (which came under the more general heading of rocking the boat). In short, I wasn't getting anywhere. In retrospect, my productivity was astounding (sickening?), but such everyday hustling was just to pay my overhead and, if I was lucky, keep from going into arrears on my taxes.

The problem of course was that I was born without capital and would not be inheriting any. In taking stock of my situation I realized that my intention of using general-purpose journalism to support my private writing was not working well. The income from the former, and the workload involved, fluctuated so wildly as I went in and out of favour from month to month that it vacuumed up valuable energy needed for the latter. As I look back now, scanning my bookshelves, I can easily see when scrambling for a living left me time for sustained work of my own (a book of prose published that year) and when it left me only a few hours at a time (ending, ultimately, in a collection of poems, the result of a long process that involved letting the surfaces dry thoroughly between each application of lacquer). I was in my high twenties now but it was not too late, I hoped, to reformulate my plans. The first order of business would be to stop paying two rents (home, and the office at Vera's place) and consolidate in a house in which I could accumulate equity. Barring some unexpected bounty, that seemed the only thing that would save me in the long run. I was right, of course. No major windfall has yet befallen me. But I have experienced runs of good luck, when the well-oiled tumblers of chance have silently aligned themselves to my advantage. Indeed, one such visitation had already begun without my realizing it.

For single persons to buy houses was not so common then as it became later. People still thought in terms of male/female couples as the basic and permanent social unit. Paradoxically, the trend towards single occupancy rose at the same time as the realization of just how difficult it would be to carry a mortgage and otherwise support a downtown household on the salary of one person. I had no one in my life at the moment and was not expecting anyone to emerge, for after an unnatural period of cosmetic stability I was starting to age rapidly and no longer felt myself to be sexually attractive. Despite long years in the social marketplace, I had never met a woman who wanted me to father her child (my most conspicuous failure as a human being, perhaps, but not necessarily my most profound—my feelings on this issue mutate and remutate as I get older). So I was planning on living alone. Secure in that knowledge, I set off on the housing search in a scientific frame of mind. It was 1977, during the spring, when prices are naturally higher.

I first made a mental map of where I wanted to reside—the area bounded by Bloor on the south, Bathurst on the west, Huron on the east, and the CPR right-of-way on the north. Then, for a specified period—three months, I think it was—I inspected every property that came on the market, calculating the scope of the financial difficulties inherent in each. I then plotted them on a grid and categorized them by size, sub-neighbourhood and street. Here again, the great inflation of the 1980s made such figures seem ridiculous today, but I concluded that I needed between $12,000 and $15,000 for a down payment and legal costs on one of the smaller houses in my target sector. That was a lot of money for somebody who at his most secure might have $500 in the bank. But fortune was running in my direction.

One of my neighbours on Howland Avenue was David Lewis Stein. He belonged to that generation ahead of mine that cast such a long shadow (he was a university contemporary of Peggy Atwood, Dennis Lee, David Helwig and so on). Like me, he too had spent years trying to balance imaginative writing and journalism, with the important difference that his career as a journalist had been interesting. He had worked on the *International Herald-Tribune* in Paris, for example. Later he covered the American uprisings of 1968 for the Toronto *Star*, an experience that would affect him profoundly and would result in the most deeply felt (and now hardest-to-find) of all his books,

*Living the Revolution: The Yippies in Chicago.* Dave was short, well-built, dark and lantern-jawed. He chewed on cigars and wore an old brown fedora, especially indoors. He was emotionally steeped in the history of the rapidly fading immigrant Jewish community on Spadina; intellectually, he was wrapped up with city politics and development issues, to the point of going back to school to get a degree in urban planning and joining a co-operative firm of left-wing planning consultants. Even in his many novels and short-story collections down through the years, the city itself has been the main character.

At this point, Dave was conducting a course in the urban planning programme at Ryerson Polytechnical Institute (later university). The idea was to teach future planners how to understand media coverage of their work. Dave asked me to share this course with him. As the term was coming to an end, I heard from the expatriate South African journalist Marq de Villiers, once the Moscow correspondent of the *Telegram* and one of the most pleasant, stable and even-tempered people I've ever met in the business, that another journalism faculty member was going to take a year's leave. The chore was the one of teaching the mandatory first-year survey course, called Media and Society, which I came to believe should be renamed All Previous Thought: An Introduction. Marq readily agreed to recommend me for the spot. At almost this same instant I received a lunch invitation from Sandy Ross, who had just settled in at *Canadian Business*. Sandy was not a promiscuous luncher, not with people of the same sex. Something was afoot.

In the 1970s (in high contrast to the 1980s and 1990s), financial journalism was a backwater. The big player was the dry-as-chalk Report on Business section of the *Globe and Mail*, which returned a huge profit largely from the sale of so-called tombstone ads, in which executive appointments are announced to the world. Better written was the *Financial Post*, a weekly broadsheet, but it held no appeal for the general reader except in its features section, which included a magazine (for which, inevitably, I wrote a general-interest column for a while). The third member of the troika, the *Financial Times of Canada*, was a conceptual anomaly: a weekly tabloid that would sum up the markets' movements during the preceding five days. In an age when electronic trading was just around the corner and people were beginning, just beginning, to trade around the world, following the sunrise from Tokyo to Hongkong to Sydney to Toronto to New York to London, the *Financial Times* seemed to be operating at a logical disadvantage. But Canada was becoming more prosperous and the people greedier, and there seemed room enough for all. Certainly there was room for somebody with a new idea.

Sandy explained at lunch how Roy MacLaren, a rising star in the federal Liberals, the former president of a large Canadian branch-plant ad agency and a general man-about-business, had hit on the notion of taking some sleepy business publication, steeped in the dry diction and flat appearance of the specialist press, and applying to it the slickness and broad appeal of a highly professional general-interest magazine such as

*Toronto Life.* Accordingly, MacLaren assembled a team of people, with himself in the lead and Michael de Pencier as a junior partner and Sandy holding a tiny slice of equity. They had bought *Canadian Business*, which had been published in Montreal for half a century as the organ of the Canadian Chamber of Commerce and was, not to put too fine a point on it, a dreadful periodical, one of the last repositories of the unrewritten press release and other such remnants of a simpler and more simple-minded time. The new owners had moved the assets, such as they were, into about six hundred square feet of one of Phil Greey's buildings on Front Street. So far they had put out one issue that, while it started to look a little lame after only a few weeks, nonetheless showed the potential of MacLaren's idea. Sandy asked me if I wanted to be managing editor. Thinking of my house project, I said yes. Friends such as Fulford were quick to guffaw at the thought of my being involved in a business publication. But nothing had changed for me. Indeed, I was still on the board of *Canadian Forum*, the socialist monthly. The job for Sandy was one I undertook strictly for the money.

I now had two full-time positions. I figured that if I could stick them out for a year, living on one salary and saving the other, I'd be able to make the down payment on an Annex house and even furnish the place. (My household goods consisted mainly of book cases and filing cabinets, as well as an old desk I had acquired after the closure of the *Telegram*. Generations of newshounds had incised the numbers of long-dead police sergeants into its top surface, using the kind of sharp implements that Fulford thought people who worked on the *Tely* should never have been allowed to possess, for their own sake as well as ours.)

I write about Sandy gingerly and with sheepishness. Many of the people I most respect in journalism thought he was a wonderful fellow, and I have considerable admiration for his son Alec, who used to visit the *Canadian Business* office when he was a kid and grew up to become a writer and journalist himself; we worked together in Kingston years later. But to observe Sandy at work from my perspective—and I draw no wider conclusions from this—was to live in a state of frustration at a transparently false easygoing manner that masked a genuine lack of organizational skill. That, and his sharpness when the cut-throat businessman showed through the bohemian façade.

Before I could even commence the job, for example, Sandy took me out for a second lunch to say that I could still have the gig at the same salary but that he had decided to give the title managing editor to someone else, who would be joining us in a few minutes. The third diner presently came charging in. He turned out to be an American business writer with family ties to the U.S. intelligence community, as they say. He had been living in Canada for some time but tended to mispronounce the names of the cities where he had resided. In the event, he did very little editing and no managing, though when he wrote, which was not so often as Sandy had expected, he produced good solid stuff, albeit without much understanding of Canada. He was an Ivy League entrepreneur, always hungry for a big strike that would make him a quick fortune. One of his plans was for a rival business magazine. He kept his scheme secret but made the mistake of approaching a potential investor who sat on de Pencier's board, upstairs. Roy MacLaren had to fire him.

MacLaren was much more like a European business person than a North American one, a *Financial Times* of London reader, I would say, rather than a *Forbes* or *Fortune* type. He was an educated and sophisticated individual for whom business was just one compartment of a full life. He wrote books on Canadian historical subjects, he collected art, even painted a little himself. He had grown up in B.C., and once a year he went on retreat to a primitive mountain-top there, to cleanse his spirit. He had a humanist education, acquired at UBC and Cambridge, as well as a managerial one, acquired at Harvard. He dressed in Savile Row suits but rode to and from work on a bicycle. His elaborate manners and his complex subtleties recalled his training in External Affairs, the old External Affairs where well-roundedness was a virtue. Roy always wore bow-ties, whose semiotic meaning was different from those worn by John Fraser: Roy's, I suspect, were a tiny *hommage* to Lester Pearson. Roy must have been something of a *Wunderkind* at External, for he let drop once that he had spent several hours sitting in on a meeting with John F. Kennedy in the Oval Office. As he was forty-two when he reinvented *Canadian Business*, he could only have been in his twenties during the Kennedy administration. He served in Prague, at the U.N. in New York and, interestingly, in Saigon. In fact, he had met his formidable, aristocratic and charming wife, Lee, an economist who hailed from the former Confederate States, when she held the equivalent position in the U.S. embassy in Saigon to the one he had at the Canadian embassy. What a courtship that must have been. She spoke I don't know how many languages and was now head of fund-raising for the University of Toronto. I'll wager the well-heeled alums had difficulty saying no to her.

Unfortunately, though, I wasn't working for Roy directly but for Sandy. Since the managing editor did no managing, no managing got done. I quickly fell into the role of staff writer and rewrite man. The latter was a necessary function, since much of the stuff Sandy commissioned was from non-professionals. One of the columnists, for example, was an attractive young female economist at a chartered bank. Her copy, once pried from her inarticulate fingers, always turned out to be incomprehensible, so much so that it couldn't even be translated. I would have to go to her apartment and interview her, try to get at what she meant to covey and then write the piece myself. Sandy was partial to attractive female contributors and in several cases (though not that of the economist) made what seemed to me the egregious error of mixing business with pleasure.

Basically, I was the only person rewriting anything, and the job kept me stepping, especially when combined with my duties at Ryerson. I got up at dawn in order to be at *Canadian Business* by seven, before anyone else arrived, so as to get a head start on the stack of mind-numbing prose that had to be made entertaining. As I was completely alone in the office for a couple of hours each morning, I would have to answer the phones as well. Many of the calls were personal ones for Sandy. So many in fact that I made up special "While You Were Out" forms, which I would leave on his desk. *Ms* [fill in name] *called at* [fill in time] *to say . . ."* There were then choices to be checked off, such as *She never wants to see you again* or *Get your goddam clothes out of her apartment.* Or *Other.* (But never *All of the above.* He was, after all, my boss.)

By prearrangement, I would slip out at about nine to rush to my morning class. It took place in an auditorium filled with about 150 young people who, to my horror, kept addressing me as sir. Ryerson's journalism programme grew respectable later on, after Don Obe became its chair and put the place on a professional footing. In my time, however, the head was Dick Lunn, husband of Janet Lunn, the beloved writer of young-adult fiction. Dick was a footnote in journalistic history, because it was to him, then a stringer for *Time*, that Roy Thomson made his only famous remark—the one about how owning the Scottish television licence was like having a licence to print money. As an educator, Dick followed the path of least resistance. He was under enormous pressure from the administration to accept as many students as possible, for the sake of tuition revenue. Accordingly, the raw talent was woefully uneven. On the one hand, there was a student who had so recently arrived from Guinea-Bissau that she didn't have enough command of English to understand what was said in class, much less read the textbooks and do the exercises. Why on earth was she in journalism? On the other hand, there were many bright people of every race and background who were eager to lap up even more than I could give them and, to no one's surprise, went on to be the next generation of quality Canadian journalists. One was David Olive, whom I helped get a job as *Toronto Life* fact-checker on graduation and who went on to become the editor of the *Report on Business Magazine* at the *Globe*. Others ranged from Kirk LaPointe, now the head of Southam News, to Kirk Makin, the distinguished justice reporter of the *Globe*, to Daphne Bramham, the Vancouver *Sun*'s Pacific Rim columnist, to Bob McKenzie, the hockey critic of the Toronto *Star*. Wendy Mesley, the future CBC news anchor, was already working in broadcasting and would arrive in class even more bleary-eyed than I was, having just put in the night-shift at CHIN, the multi-lingual radio station. The students came from across the country, and I found that, on balance and despite the levelling influence of television, the ones from urban backgrounds had a natural advantage over those from small-town and rural areas simply in terms of overall sophistication and the amount of general information they possessed. The real performers were naturally the so-called mature students, who had already taken a B.A. somewhere and were coming into the programme simply for technical grounding in what they had now decided would be their career. An example is Paula Brook, later my friend and for years the editor of *Western Living* in Vancouver.

After these sessions in the Ryerson auditorium I would race back to my role as cipher clerk at *Cana-*

*dian Business* and work through lunch. Then, twice a week, I would scoot back up to Ryerson, urging the driver not to spare the horses, and conduct two sessions of classroom and lab work each time. Which meant that I would then return to the magazine and, in order to put in my full eight hours, work there long after everyone else had left. Then I would go home myself and begin to correct students' papers or make a lesson-plan for the next day, often only to fall asleep exhausted in front of *Charlie's Angels* or some other idiotic emblem of 1970s television culture. It didn't take many months of this grind to wear me down. Here I was twenty-eight years old getting chest pains from the stress of working two unpleasant jobs, one of which was getting worse.

One day Sandy returned from one of the pawn-shops on lower Church Street with a fistful of obscure military medals, some on ribbons, others just on pins, and made a ceremony of awarding them to the four or five of us in the editorial office, one to each, and kissing us on the cheek like a French general. Another time he suddenly walked to the centre of the editorial coop, went down on the floor and then stood on his head, straight as a lodgepole pine, to emphasize some point he was making, I can't begin to imagine what it was. To illustrate his hipness and his playful side, Sandy kept a classic pinball machine next to his desk. It had an electrical short he could never quite keep fixed, and so the machine tended to catch fire from time to time, filling the office with the smell of burning insulation. Once a week we were supposed to draw our chairs in a semi-circle round his desk while he put his feet up on his work-surface and convened the editorial meeting. On at least one occasion he got the meeting off to a certain start by whipping out his tenor banjo to accompany himself in singing an obscure American country tune from the early 1950s entitled "When Jesus Tears the Iron Curtain Down."

I must say his story sense was terrific. He had a wonderful ability to pluck ideas out of thin air and to detect editorial flaws in other people's, almost before they had been let onto the agenda. What was wrong was his manner, the result possibly of the conflict he lived out between his public style and his private politics. He generally divided stories into two categories, *hard cock* and *soft cock*, sometimes in the writers' hearing. And he had strange prejudices. He became convinced, for example, that I was gay because I stuttered. Now if I were, I'd be proudly gay, but he was simply mistaken. I knew a little something about speech pathology, about how down through history people who stuttered were thought to be possessed by devils or how they had become Freudian case studies, and everything in between; in the eighteenth century, for example, stuttering was misdiagnosed as simple forgetfulness. Nowhere, however, had I run into Sandy's theory, one from which I couldn't dissuade him. He would sometimes lean over my desk and make some crude homophobic joke, expecting me to—actually, I'm not sure what he expected. Perhaps that I'd challenge him to a duel by slapping his silly face with a scented handkerchief, suitably embroidered. For one reason or another, he always stopped at my desk every time he either entered or left the office, emitting the impression that I was slacking. In fact, I was processing most of the copy, as a look through those old issues proves to me. Only Steve Manly, the highly talented art director, worked harder. One problem, I suppose, was that we didn't have enough people. Roy MacLaren's concept was certainly the right one for the time. Circulation and advertising were to double quite easily in the first four years, but in the initial year there was still no budget for staff. And Sandy may have resented that I was doing two jobs, though we had talked this out at the beginning and he had been encouraging. Indeed, when I had trouble getting a bank to give me a mortgage, he contacted "a guy I know" in Barrie, who had no qualms at all, and at a competitive rate. I would say that he seemed not to like me much, if it weren't for contrary evidence in the form of such acts of kindness. I suspect that, although he had once been managing editor of *Maclean's* and seemed easy-going to people who met him casually, he wasn't comfortable in the role of boss, which demands both a close scrutiny and a gift for the overview: a combination he wasn't able to bring into alignment or was unable to maintain for long enough.

After a year of doing both jobs, I was a wreck ("How could he tell?" I hear readers asking), but at least (and at last) I had my house. I was getting set to move on (and move in) when two events occurred that imparted a slightly bitter taste to the whole *Canadian Business* experience.

The industry had recently got together to begin a foundation that would present the first National

Magazine Awards. Hedley had submitted my long piece on the *Globe and Mail*, which made it to the short list in the general best-article category. One afternoon I walked into the open-plan *CB* office to hear Sandy in a deep phone conversation with some-one, I couldn't tell who, about "the Fetherling prob-lem." He was skittish afterwards but told me he had just been informed that some grass-roots movement had taken shape to protest the probability that this key award would be going to someone born in the U.S. My first thought was that this was a double-reverse whammy originating in the rumour mill at the U.S. consulate, though 1978 was pretty late in the day for the people there to still be trying to under-mine me with tricks and visitations, as they had done sometimes in the past—but only randomly, never in an organized way. No, the problem had some other source, I felt sure. Stephen Franklin, the head of the foundation, would confirm that he had received many "complaints" about my being short-listed but didn't feel that I had a right to any more information than that. I questioned him about what the judging procedures were. He allowed that the judges did not meet one another but sent their votes separately to him for tabulation, without anyone looking over his shoulder.

Wearing my good sportsmanship on the sleeve of my hired tuxedo, I duly turned up for the gala evening in a hotel ballroom. The emcee announced that the best-article award had gone to a piece about a sportswriter's visit to a dairy farm. A sustained boo went up from the crowd in my support, which I regretted as the winning piece was rather well done and its author didn't deserve to be caught in the middle this way. Later in the evening I saw Dic Doyle of the *Globe*, who it seemed to me rarely ventured out to such social occasions, standing with a small group. I went up and said how nice it was to see him again. He grinned like a mortician. Since then my attitude towards awards and prizes has been this: never seek them, never refuse them, never wear them in public before 8:00 p.m.

The other happening was a dreadful error at the magazine. Although I worked on most of the copy, and did a post-mortem on the issues, I didn't do production—the reading of first proofs, corrected proofs and finally vandykes. Sandy and his assistant did that, while the art department made sure the ads were where they should be. As the ad deadline fell later in the month than the editorial deadline (in order to scoop up any last-minute insertions), there was always the slight danger of something going wrong if the person ultimately responsible wasn't paying close attention. The inevitable happened. One month there was a major feature story that jumped from page E to continue on page F, from where it was to conclude on page Y. Except that on page Y there was an ad rather than the ending of the story, which was left to dangle, like a murder mystery without the concluding scene. Roy MacLaren was understandably furious with Sandy. After a day of vigorous contrition to the writer of the piece and the advertising community, he was heard to say that something must be done.

The only answer, it was clear to me, was to hire

somebody to be a managing editor who would actually manage—revamp procedures as needed and take responsibility, actually signing off the art boards to indicate that they were error-free and ready for the camera. Sandy knew I was right. I went on to say that I thought I knew of the perfect person. I had known Margaret Wente since she was in a junior position as a publicist at Doubleday on Bond Street. We had worked together on a couple of projects at *The Canadian* and the CBC. One time I set her up in a lucrative book deal, indeed had helped to find her a place to live, and I knew her to be just the kind of glutton for detail we needed. As she was now editing the Royal Ontario Museum members' magazine, I thought she could be lured away. Sandy said no, he'd never heard of her and he wasn't sure "this girl" (she was almost my age) would be right. But as he didn't have any candidates of his own, I pressed her case forward and he eventually hired her. At the conclusion of her *first day* on the job, while still meeting people and learning what was where, she came over to my desk, put her hands on her hips and said to my face, "Well, *some* people around here are certainly overpaid."

What had happened, I suppose, is that in one day Sandy saw that I was right about Wente—and guessed that she could do my work too. But he didn't fire me. Rather he just stopped talking to me for a couple of weeks until, unable to put it off any longer, he sort of shyly asked me not to come in any more. Roy MacLaren seemed embarrassed by the whole affair and took it upon himself to pay me the same severance package he had given the original "managing editor" whom he had had to fire. Thanking him for this, I made some remark about Sandy. Roy sympathized but said, "Sandy has rare talents and sometimes you have to give an exceptionally free hand to people like that." They were making each other rich.

I was pissed off, not at Roy, whom I continue to like and admire, but at commercial journalism, at the system, at forever being either the good cop or bad cop. Anyway, I was out of work about a day and a half, just long enough for a really good restorative sleep. The job of supply teaching at Ryerson had come to an end, and I was able to fill in for Marq de Villiers himself, who was taking a leave from his seminar in magazine writing—a much lighter and more pleasant load than I'd been used to. After a while, my gloom lifted. As for Peggy Wente, she would soon enough become editor of *Canadian Business* herself, then editor of the *Globe*'s *Report on Business Magazine* and finally of the all-powerful RoB section itself, the very heart of the paper. A supremely competent person—just as I had convinced Sandy she was—but not, I think now, someone who really likes writers much, to judge from my subsequent encounters with her too.

---

The polar opposite of Margaret Wente was Anne Collins, a writer's editor—and a writer's writer, too, for her award-winning books, which lay in the future, would be scrupulous and painstaking attempts at coming to terms with moral issues and righting public wrongs. For Anne, somewhat like Bob Fulford, had a strong ethical sense without being in the least moralistic. This set her apart from so many other WASPs and Scots in Toronto (a place where, as I like to explain to foreign visitors, the leftover puritanism of the nineteenth century is still felt so strongly that, even today, many of our crack-houses remain closed on Sundays). Maybe Anne escaped all of that by virtue of having been reared on a farm. Frankly, though, this biographical fact used to strike me as incongruous during the first years of our acquaintanceship, for in addition to her intellectual allure she was tall, elegant, glamorous and sophisticated, with cheekbones as well defined as those seen on the sort of brass mediaeval tomb-effigies from which tourists take rubbings. But she doesn't have any of the hauteur that usually comes with.

Anne too had started out as a book publicist and then had floated up through *Chatelaine* and the rotos to a position at *Maclean's*, where she was in charge of arts coverage and other back-of-the-book departments. This was in the period after October 1975 when, under Peter Newman, the magazine had made the difficult leap from general-interest monthly to fortnightly to Canada's first full-fledged news weekly. Peter seemed to me to possess a broad streak of libertarianism. He didn't wish *Maclean's*, like every other newsmagazine from *Time* on up the scale, to be written in a single tone of voice. He thought it should be a forum where writers exercised some individuality as to viewpoint and prose. As for staff relations, those who worked for him often mistook his shyness and his quiet style of leadership for incitement to run amok. The result was quite an interesting magazine to read, full of ups and downs, and a rather strange one for which to work.

As a weekly now, *Maclean's* was an insatiable market for freelance contributions, and at various points during this stretch I must have written for most sections of the magazine. But as Peter's lines of authority were so blurred, the lowliest member of the staff could influence how a piece was displayed or even whether it was used at all. Instead of one boss—the fellow who sat in the huge office in the centre of a white horseshoe-shaped desk, smoking his pipe—you had a score of bosses, warring with one another and with you. I offer two examples. Peter sent me a memo asking me to do a business story about some specific entrepreneurs in the Canadian film industry, which was undergoing one of its periodic boomlets. Peter was giving out this assignment since the business editor, a former small-city newspaper reporter of immature bearing, was away. The piece I turned in was accepted. Then the business editor returned from his holiday and picked a fight with Peter, saying that if the piece ran he would quit. Not being able to find a new business editor on a Friday afternoon, Peter, apologizing to me, killed the piece. That night, the business editor telephoned me, perhaps a little drunkenly (I give him the benefit of the doubt), to denounce me as a disgrace to the honourable trade of journalism, etc. He disappeared from *Maclean's* soon afterwards, following one or two similar snits perhaps, to enter public relations, never to be heard from again. Another time Peter wanted me to do a story on politics in Bermuda. I talked to officials and civilians both Black and white and interviewed Sir Edwin Leather, originally of Hamilton, Ontario, latterly of Hamilton, Bermuda, where he had stayed on after retirement, following an unprecedented second term as governor of the colony. Peter thought the piece was fine. But it was killed by a fact-checker who, though I doubt he'd ever been to Bermuda, disagreed with my statement that race relations there had improved considerably since the low-point in March 1973, when Sir Edwin's predecessor, Sir Dickie Sharples, had been foully murdered. On one occasion I was unofficially banished from the magazine for being unco-operative in the face of ignorant chaos. Another of the section editors (I won't embarrass him by giving his name, as I have reason to believe that he's grown smarter with age) asked me to write, in the Media section to which I often contributed, a story on airline magazines. Weeks later he telephoned in a panic to say that there were things in the copy he couldn't understand, urgent uncertainties that would have to be resolved in person during the next half-hour so that he could move the copy. When I arrived, panting, at his office in the Maclean Hunter building at University and Dundas, his questions turned out to be two in number.

"Why," he wanted to know, "do advertisers buy space in these airline magazines?"

I looked him up and down just to make sure he wasn't pulling my leg. Then I replied calmly, "In order to sell their goods and services."

He duly wrote down this fact.

"The other question is here on page two, where

you say that the volume of passenger traffic is heaviest around Christmas and New Year's. Why would that be?"It shames me to say that I walked out of his office rather than waste on him any more of the rock-like patience for which I was justly renowned.

Most of the staff was poorly paid. Some had been cobbled together from God knows where. Still another of the section editors, for instance, had been running a boutique when Peter suddenly plucked her out of retail for a life in journalism. In the resulting atmosphere of confusion, there was always something pleasant and reassuring about dealing with natural pros such as Anne Collins. A special example of her tact has stayed with me.

The flamboyant American actress Elizabeth Ashley, who had worked in Canada and was married to a Canadian, had just published her memoirs, a breathless and meaty work. Anne asked me if I would have dinner with her for the purpose of doing a short interview. Anyone who's been pretending to be a journalist as long as I have has inevitably had meals with many famous people and has come to distrust if not also dislike, as I have, the very concept of celebrity. I can say honestly, and with unflinching acknowledgement of the person I used to be, that being in the same room with Big Bill Lias—*El Grande,* lord of charisma—ruined my faculty for awe. Seeing Bob Dylan at a party and shaking hands with the British prime minister, much less putting questions to movie stars, couldn't compete with that.

Ashley was staying where all such visitors stayed in those days, the Windsor Arms on St Thomas

Street. I was summoned upstairs to find her sitting cross-legged on the bed talking with a young publicity rep from the Canadian publisher that was distributing her book here. We had some tequila while she fielded a few phone calls and talked to me a bit in between: the scene was very familiar from the example of others who carry their lives with them on the road. Finally, I went downstairs to the Courtyard Café (a *boîte* on civilization, I once heard myself call it) and waited there while Ashley changed. She finally swept into the dining room, still accompanied by the PR. She wore a kind of see-through Victorian dress. When I'd interviewed celebs there in the past, the café staff had always seated us back towards the kitchen, well out of sight of those coming and going. But Ashley insisted on the biggest table and the one nearest the entrance, I didn't know why—yet. Every fourth person who came into the room, it seemed, was somebody she knew or felt she ought to know, someone who should be invited to join us. First came a local rocker I'd seen around town for years but never spoken to. Then a chap who owned some after-hours clubs. Then the sister of the first fellow, who was working as an assistant to the producer on a film written by Tom Hedley. Then Pierre Sarrazin, the brother of the actor Michael Sarrazin and his exact double, perhaps his twin. Then two Broadway big-shots in their fifties who had come to Canada to rent one of the theatres at Stratford for some off-season rehearsals. I can't recall who else. Ashley invited each in turn to join us and kept calling for more champagne.

I barely managed to interject a couple of interview-style questions. Mainly what I seemed to be getting on tape was the soundtrack of a riotous private party. Ashley, I remember, kept speaking of putting *energy* back into the *system* lest she risk a smack (she looked heavenward) from the Big Paw, her affectionate name for God. She *became* a Tennessee Williams character when tipsy, which is the condition in which we all quickly found ourselves.

Ashley spoke repeatedly of being thirty-nine and of growing up in the 1960s. It was sad to observe her highly charged melancholy and see the effects of her continuous attempt to subdue it in creating youthful exuberance. But she was another of those remarkably ionizing women: smart, ballsy, a tangle of uncertainties and confusions but no less positive an example because of them.

When the Courtyard closed, and I'd been stuck with the bill, we all returned to her room. The goings-on were still going on when in the middle of the night someone sent out for mind-benders. I left before they were delivered. The next day, or later that morning, I should say, I had to go to Anne Collins and explain, through my headache, why it was that I was submitting to *Maclean's* a champagne tab for $355, or considerably more than the fee for the piece.

"Dom Perignon 1970," I remember saying weakly. "Luckily for us the Courtyard doesn't stock an even better vintage."

Rather than risk putting my chit past Peter, Anne promised to tack onto each of my next ten assignments an additional hidden fee of $35.50, which she did. I also think she may have found me some codeine in her desk. In those days, codeine was a staple foodstuff at *Maclean's*.

———————

Those were boom-times in journalism, much more so than we who were trapped in the belly of the beast could appreciate. Boom-times meant start-ups and failures as well as days of consolidated success. People took chances trying to seize the mood of the moment. A few made it; many didn't. Some American and Canadian magazines that went under in the 1970s, or at least began their terminal decline during that decade, may bring back the flavour to those who remember the names: *Bookviews, Energy, New Times, More, Scanlan's* (successor to *Ramparts*), *Viva, Quest*. People were coming in and out of the business all the time, and I found that on occasion I could get work as a consultant, giving quick intensive seminars to people who, for one reason or another, suddenly found themselves in positions of greater authority than their actual experience could support. When a Liberal senator's daughter who worked at *Quill & Quire* found herself its new editor, without having risen up the ranks anywhere else, she kindly asked me to teach her such matters as elementary layout and design and the delicate art, as old as Gutenberg, of getting along with printers. I was delighted to accept.

# What Happened
# Next

THE BOOZE started to catch up with Hugh Garner in the mid-1970s, and once it took over his system, the decline was pretty steep. He turned to those detective novels, each one a little less competent than the last, until in the end he planned to kill off Inspector McDumont in a final thriller. The manuscript was unfinished at his death and was later reworked and completed by his biographer, Paul Stuewe: an unusual collaboration between the living and the dead.

My last talks with Garner were on the phone when it was becoming clear that memory loss had been added to his list of medical difficulties. He had trouble with common words. "When I was working on *Liberty* in the fifties," he said, "old So-and-so was my—what do you call it? Hell's fire, he was the before-guy . . ."

"Predecessor," I said. I shouldn't have, but he didn't seem to notice or to mind.

"Yeah, yeah. Predecessor." He pushed on until the

next lapse a moment later. In a subsequent call, he couldn't remember Jack Kent Cooke's name.

During this period one kept hearing alarming stories that he had broken his own long-standing rule and was now going on sprees even though he was working on a piece of writing. Then the news would come that he was in hospital. One heard occasionally that some new malady, such as kidney failure or the loss of feeling in his legs, had brought him perilously close to the end. Yet he always seemed to recover.

The last time I spoke with him was on a diplomatic mission of sorts. Don Obe, who was by now the editor of *Toronto Life*, had commissioned him to write a memoir of the Canadian National Exhibition but was hearing some particularly discouraging rumours about his alcohol intake. The deadline was very near. Would I, Don asked, get in touch with him and subtly bring the conversation round to the article? Had he remembered to work on it at all? Was there any hope of it being in on time?

I called, fearing it would be one of those dreadful situations one experiences as a young reporter: using some pretext to interview the grand old man for his file obituary, knowing that he knows the true purpose of the talk and that you know that he knows. But it wasn't like that at all. The conversation was long, discursive and one-sided: a disjointed ramble through past times and past feuds. Feuds with *editors*? I asked hopefully. Oh yeah, damn right, goddam editors. I mentioned a few including Don Obe, but the conversation shifted to somebody else before he got the sentence out. I brought up the topic again, more cleverly,

I thought, and then a third time. "Oh yeah, did I tell you?" he said at last, jamming the information between other thoughts. "Obe asked me to do this piece for him. I almost got it done." Then he careened onwards. I sighed inwardly, mission accomplished. The article was his last published journalism. It would be instructive perhaps to look it up and compare it with the *Canadian Forum* article on the CNE he mentions in his autobiography as being the earliest piece of writing he ever got published. My guess is that his first and his last credits in a forty-some-year career would turn out to be remarkably similar, a secret I'm sure he was keeping from Don Obe.

On June 18, 1979, the *Globe* reported that Garner was critically ill in hospital, the first time that such an occurrence, by now common, was picked up by the press. I feared the worst. Then he seemed to recover. But no, the situation grew quite dangerous again. He died some time round midnight on June 30. According to the papers, his last words, spoken to Mrs Garner from an oxygen tent, were, "Alice, get me another drink."

I went to the funeral with Bob Fulford and remember being slightly surprised to discover that Garner had been an Anglican. I had always assumed somehow that his people in the West Riding of Yorkshire had been dissenters of one stripe or another, and I'm sure that he hadn't simply graduated to Anglicanism once he got successful (as the Masseys, for example, had done). Anyway, some of the literary people and publishers he quarrelled with the most violently turned up. I remember Jack McClelland being there, for instance. So, according to a TV report later, was at least one fellow Spanish Civil War vet. But the most fitting and most fittingly sentimental fact about the ceremony was the presence of a number of anonymous and unkempt individuals. There was one in an apparently second-hand suit that didn't fit him too well, another in a salvage raincoat and very much in need of a shave. They didn't sign the guest book and no one appeared to know who they were, but they remembered Garner. They were people from his stories.

Obe had succeeded to the editorship of *Toronto Life* after the independent-minded Tom Hedley ("He's never been a company man," Obe once said to me admiringly) gave up magazines to write screenplays. His first script, adapted from a Ross MacDonald novel, became *Double Negative* (1979), with Susan Clark, Kate Reid and a Hedley buddy, Michael Sarrazin. Its release followed a period of uncertainty caused by the tragic early death of the producer. Next was *Circle of Two* (1980), with Tatum O'Neal and Richard Burton; it was eventually purchased by cable after the production company went bankrupt. Premature bankruptcy also hindered *Mr Patman*, a 1981 pastiche from the director of the *King Kong* remake, starring Kate Nelligan and James Coburn. That same year, Hedley moved to Hollywood, where he netted a million dollars with a script entitled *Flashdance*, one of the signal box office scores of the early 1980s. He bought a BMW and a 1960 mint-condition, cream-coloured Cadillac.

Office politics at *Maclean's* never settled down. Indeed, they grew ever more fractious. Peter Newman's editorship, which had begun in 1971, lasted until 1981: a crucial period. It came to an end when some of the most vicious office-politickers, who enjoyed his patronage but constantly took advantage of his low-key style of leadership, secretly organized a chapter of the Newspaper Guild at the magazine. Peter resigned as editor and stepped up his production as a best-selling author but remained on the Maclean Hunter board for years and still writes a column in the magazine each week. He was succeeded as editor by an intense fellow indeed, who after what seemed an eternity was followed in turn by one of Newman's former top people, Robert Lewis, who began the difficult job of getting the magazine facing the right way again.

Affairs at *Saturday Night* went from comic-opera to melodrama. As the decade turned, Ed Cowan was out as publisher, having kept the magazine alive and in new clothing but having failed to make it the runaway success all of us had once envisioned so optimistically. Ed returned to the mercurial world of independent arts and media entrepreneurs but was never so prominent again. Norman Webster, by now Dic Doyle's successor as editor of the *Globe and Mail*, assumed ownership of the magazine, or rather, headed the Webster family holding company that did so. In December 1979—end of the decade, a new beginning—he brought in as publisher John Macfarlane, whom I had worked with when he'd been editor of *Weekend*, *Toronto Life* (the first time), and so on, back to the days when he had just been taken on at the Toronto *Star* on King Street, when he was in his late twenties and I was a teenager. The following year the magazine moved yet again, to 70 Bond Street, the old Macmillan of Canada building where I used to tease the telephonist, and later still to a large multi-storey designer-created space at 511 King Street West, which Fulford called "probably the first address that *Saturday Night* has had in decades and decades that was right in the middle of where the creative action is in the city." But Bob was not a happy individual during this period. One could see as much on his countenance and hear it in his voice.

Except for the all-important difference that he is not in the least sinister (and has always improved whatever he's touched), John Macfarlane nonetheless has frequently reminded me of the line in Allen Ginsberg's "Howl" about "the mustard gas of sinister intelligent editors." For he was indeed intelligent. And he was at all times surrounded by an invisible gaseous cloud of personal and professional slickness. Between magazines, Macfarlane, who was probably one of the best-dressed men of his age in Toronto, had held high positions in advertising and in television. Such jobs only underscored what was obvious to those of us who saw him from the inside: that he was a visual person more than a word person. He had a rare talent for spotting young designers right out of art college or even before. It is a testament to his eye for horseflesh that *Saturday Night* would have a succession of art directors who were stolen away by the rustlers at *Rolling Stone, Vanity Fair, Esquire* and *GQ*.

Yet Macfarlane held equally strong views about writers and writing, though he tended to pick one or two staff people and a couple of favourite freelancers and rely on them again and again to an unusual degree. For example, he put great store in Gary Ross as an editor and would bring him into whatever editorial situation he occupied at the moment. Ross, who had independent means derived from gambling and who aspired to be a novelist and screenwriter, was indeed a talented fellow. But the two of them together seemed to cook up a house cadence for *Saturday Night* prose that not everyone could master to their satisfaction but anybody could mimic. It had a dissonant sound: ta, ta, ta, ta, boom, *ta* ta—ta. Repeated endlessly in long articles about business executives and politicians of the moment—the new staples of *Saturday Night*—it proved deadly to the reader's ear and patience. But then Macfarlane and Ross also gave the world that wonderful prose writer David Macfarlane (no relation). For some reason I could never understand, probably a misplaced cosmopolitan urge, Macfarlane also took an unalterable fancy to the work of Jan Morris, perhaps the world's most formula-bound and most tiresome travel writer.

There were rumours when Macfarlane and Ross took over that Fulford was on his way out. But the parties obviously reached some sort of silent accommodation, and I can guess what it would have been. Bob was dreadfully unhappy having to do anything on the business side of the magazine; I think he probably preferred going to the dentist's to shaking hands with an advertiser or thinking about a purely business question. In exchange for giving up some of the editorial freedom he had enjoyed in the old days on York Street and St Clair—that is, by moving the magazine away from arts and culture, towards finance and politics—he was relieved of all the onerous stuff he dreaded and despised. In the trade, he ended up with more time for his own writing, and he began to do long features for the island. The ones that most accurately suited his temperament, such as a piece on Dic Doyle of the *Globe*, were some of the most finely crafted articles in the magazine.

One day in June 1987 I telephoned Fulford to congratulate him on his first honorary degree, which he was to receive that day from York University.

"How are things going down there?"

"Oh fine, fine," he answered. "The magazine's just been bought by Conrad Black."

He spoke in such a level conversational tone that I thought he was kidding. But he wasn't.

"My God," I said almost without thinking. "Do you suppose you'll have to resign?"

After a pause, he replied: "I need to see what the details are, but yes, maybe that will turn out to be the best course."

Both Fulford and Black would describe what happened next in their respective memoirs, *Best Seat in the House* and *A Life in Progress*. They seemed to agree that the meeting was tense. Black filled the appointment with an old schoolmate from Upper Canada College, the loquacious Sinophile and former dance critic John Fraser, who beat out Margaret Wente and others, if the published gossip of the time is to be believed. Fraser spent the next five years living in the midst of the kind of uproar and mischief he so enjoys while he figured out how to keep the magazine alive for the succeeding generation (his answer was to switch to controlled circulation, distributing half a million copies ten times a year through certain big metropolitan newspapers, including the *Globe*). Fraser's first issue was published from yet another address, 36 Toronto Street, which would not be the magazine's last.

We who were his friends were worried about Fulford. He had been the editor for nineteen years and was fifty-five, a dangerous age. He and Geraldine took an extended trip to Japan that seemed to pique his old curiosity but couldn't disguise his sadness. "I saw Bob today," I would report to my wife or she to me, "and he was wearing his bedroom slippers again." Metaphorical bedroom slippers, we meant. I for one was not much relieved when the *Financial Times of Canada* announced that Fulford would be writing a weekly column for them. The column was excellent, of course, but wasn't that how the great B.K. Sandwell had ended up after his glorious career at *Saturday Night*, writing a column in the *Financial Post*, which was so unworthy of his talents? Later, Fulford was tapped for a succession of brass gigs. He spent a year as Barker Fairley Distinguished Visitor in Canadian Culture at the University of Toronto. The position had the charm of being named after Barker Fairley, the poet and painter who had helped to found the *Canadian Forum* in 1920 (and whom I heard remark at the *Forum*'s fiftieth-anniversary party, "If I knew the thing would last this long, I would have tried to make a better job of it"). The other advantage of the Fairley chair is that it was unencumbered by any noticeable duties, so Bob used the time to write his aforementioned memoirs. Later, he headed the arts journalism programme at the Banff Centre; later still, he taught media ethics at Ryerson.

But then he climbed up out of the slough like the deceptively sturdy person he's always been. He found that being a freelance, virtually for the first time in his life, widened his horizons. He soon had a weekly column in the *Globe* but was actually to be found all over the newsstands, writing on art, design, architecture, the zoo of politics and the zen of culture. He became an elder statesman, pestered for his response to important turning-points in the life of the nation, solicited for obituaries when his eminent elders or contemporaries dropped off the edge of the Earth. Janet and I remembered the party for his fiftieth birthday, because it was our first public date as a couple. His sixtieth was marked by a dinner with speeches by friends representing the various areas of his life. The affair was on a Sunday and happened to coincide with the first time he had a piece on the front of the *New York Times Book Review*.

He seemed that rarest of beings, a genuinely happy man. His intellectual world, instead of narrowing, grew broader. He set out to write a book about American culture in the year 1953 (the year he turned twenty-one), but it had promptly become a book called *Accidental City: The Transformation of Toronto*, which trafficked not at all in nostalgia or in Americanism but analyzed the sources of the local and the present and looked bravely into the future. By this time, to the mute astonishment of those of us who had known him so long, or thought we had, Bob had turned into a techie: his enthusiasm and natural thirst had triumphed over his lack of innate ability, and he began performing casual feats of magic with computers—a transition that defeated many a younger person.

The follow-up to Sandy Ross is more troublesome for me to write. He once again became the editor of *Canadian Business*, his shares in which had already made him well off, but his and Roy MacLaren's dream of a slick business magazine with all the readability of a consumer one came to grief with intense competition from the *Report on Business Magazine*, the *Financial Post Magazine*, *Equity* and God knows how many others. Sandy had to reposition the magazine in a more serious niche, as one full of economics and management theory not accessible to outsiders. I don't believe he had much fun doing so, but at least he stopped trying to present himself to the world as a hip guy. His hair grew shorter and grey, his outfits more serious, he forsook his funky National Health spectacles for what were probably known as power glasses. No more pinball machines or banjos.

My suspicion is that Sandy got tired of the magazine, passing it on to a series of much younger editors, but found when he went back to writing that he had run out of things to say. He wrote a couple of books about business, one of which I have reason to believe he didn't actually read. Later, he took on commissioned corporate writing, and was defensive about doing so. I am uncomfortable reporting this, because I don't enjoy treating others unkindly and am uncertain about my objectivity, since some of the people whose opinions I respect the most—Val Ross, for example—have memories of Sandy completely different from mine. I can only conclude that some flaw in my own character compelled him to keep his good side hidden from me.

"With my kind of lifestyle," Sandy said to me one day, "I'll probably die of cancer—from the cigarettes and stress." No. In 1993 he suffered a stroke. He was fifty-eight but still looked like Jack London. When I saw him last he was in a wheelchair, being helped down the aisle of a darkened cinema by Minette, his last wife. He died two months later. His funeral was as crowded as any I have ever attended. Especially conspicuous in the chapel were many women from his past, weeping. Old colleagues were hyperbolic in what they wrote about him in the magazines and papers, including the *Globe*, where Margaret Wente recalled: "I never thought of that brilliant, erratic, disorderly man as my mentor, and it's a word he never would have used. . . . But the journalistic values I absorbed from him—surprise, cheek, great storytelling and good writing—live in my bones."

Roy MacLaren, whom I'd liked at once and continue to do so, made enough money at *Canadian Business* to devote himself to public life (and to writing a few more books along the way). He became a Liberal MP and served in the cabinets of three prime ministers, Pierre Trudeau, John Turner and Jean Chrétien. He became an increasingly conservative Liberal, which troubled me. In 1996, at sixty-one, he was appointed High Commissioner to Britain. He occupies the office in Canada House in Trafalgar Square where, as a twenty-one-year-old, he had taken his oral exam to enter the foreign service.

Like Fulford, Kildare Dobbs discovered more happiness as a freelance writer than many of his friends had expected him to find. Beginning in the 1980s he basked in a new reputation as a writer of stylish book-length travel narratives dealing with places as different as Turkey and Texas. But at this writing, in 1996, he is seventy-three and recovering from a major illness.

Poor health has also plagued my friend and former colleague in mischief, Charles Taylor. While his father was alive, Charles always maintained that he wouldn't get sucked into running the family enterprises but would fulfil his destiny as an author. But long before E.P. Taylor died, in 1989, after a slow and sad decline, Charles found himself devoting more and more energy to what he called the horse business. I believe he enjoyed the equestrian world as much as he did the book world, though differently of course. Also, he found marital happiness with the painter Noreen Tomlinson. From my own conversations with him, as well as from field reports by my people on the ground, I know that he is showing incredible and not unexpected bravery in the face of a lingering disease.

As for Vera Frenkel, her partners forced her from the studio building on Davenport Road in some sort of real estate deal, but she rebounded by moving into a combined work and living space farther out in the West End.

"It's good to be able to sleep next to your work," I said to her. "It's rather the same idea as a dog sleeping close to its food and water bowls."

She agreed.

Since the move, Vera has gone from triumph to triumph as a visual artist, taking many honours and winning especially big reputations in Japan and Western Europe. But only in 1996 did she arrive at the position of being able to quit teaching at York University, after twenty-three years, to make art full time.

My old friend Nancy Naglin worked harder and harder at her writing in New York but with less and less recognition. I've too often seen what this situation can do to a person's spirit. The last time we spoke she was still living in the Village but selling real estate in Connecticut, hoping to move to L.A., where the scene is *really* weird.

But none of the above, as it took place, as it's written or as it's remembered, is in final form.

Dan Williman rebuked me recently when I pointed out that we're getting old (he's fifty-five, I'm forty-seven) and are unlikely to have many more adventures together of the sort we had in the 1970s.

"The issue has not yet gone to probate," he said.